Personalised Learning: Taking Choice Seriously

Edited by
Mark Webster

A book in the series community/creativity/choice/change

Educational Heretics Press

Published 2008 by Educational Heretics Press
113 Arundel Drive, Bramcote, Nottingham NG9 3FQ

British Cataloguing in Publication Data

Personalised learning: taking choice seriously
1.Individualsied instruction
I. Webster, Mark
371.3'94

ISBN-13:   978-1-900219-36-5

Design and production: Educational Heretics Press

Cover design by John Haxby

Printed by Adlard Print Limited, Ruddington, Nottingham

Contents

Introduction

by Mark Webster

"Personalised learning has the potential to transform our systems of learning. It challenges the shallow version of learning promoted within the present education system and proposes a new approach where learners themselves make both rational and intuitive choices about their learning. Taking choice seriously is the key driver in this choice. The prize is a cohesive, sustainable and productive society with active and democratically competent citizens."
(Publicity leaflet for the Conference *Personalised Education: Taking Choice Seriously*, held at Staffordshire University on June 25th 2007)

At the age of 7 my music teacher made me stand up in front of the class and whistle a tune she first played on the piano. Apparently my attempts were not up to her standards since after that day I was never allowed to sing in the school choir or have music lessons in school. Schools and the greater part of the education system in general, treat learning in the way that this music teacher treated my appreciation and love for music. I was not asked what tune I wanted to whistle, nor what I felt about being made to stand up in front of my peers and perform. I was not even consulted about whether or not my ability to whistle was the way I wanted a decision to be made about my future access to a music education. This arbitrary judgement made about me at the age of 7 excluded me from participating in the music life of that and my subsequent schools, and transmitted to me that I was not musical. A fact I held to be true until I learned to sing and play guitar in my teenage years.

The concept of Personalised Learning takes as its starting point that the learner knows best and that given the right support and encouragement they can determine there own learning styles and learning needs. In its conception it is anti-authoritarian as much as it is anti-institutional and as such it runs counter to the very basis of *modern* educational theory and practice. Mass education as implemented by most governments throughout the world, on the other hand, follows basically the same methodology and assumptions as my old music teacher. That is, that knowledge is something that is indisputable. It is passed down from the teacher to the taught, and learners either have the predisposition to learn it or they do not. The teacher is the one who has the power and the right to judge both the ability and the achievement of the learner. It is also something that usually happens at a predefined time in a predefined place where the learner either agrees or is cajoled into following the rules, uniforms and conventions of the institution. Choice, where it exists, is merely between options offered by the system, and usually is limited by the institution's judgement about what is suitable for the learner.

Strangely enough, this *modern* educational system has maintained its popularity and tightened its grip at a time when we have more access to information than ever before. Indeed this authoritarian version of knowledge and its acquisition co-exists with the most democratic access there has ever been to information via the computer and the World Wide Web. We live in a 24 hour, 365 day a year, information-rich society. You cannot only go on-line to read a book, but also you can go into a chat room and question the author.

In fact, you can write and distribute your own books or songs or poems.

This book was conceived as a way to put forward another version of what a modern education system might look like, one that really does take choice seriously. It does not promote one alternative, but embraces a whole range of alternatives. It is rooted in practical, ongoing work and aims to show that Personalised Learning is not just a theoretical construct that challenges the basis of mass education but consists of a whole range of practical approaches directed by learners.

The project grew out of a conference in June 2007 that was hosted by the Creative Communities Unit (CCU) at Staffordshire University and developed in a partnership between the Centre for Personalised Education Trust (CPE) and the CCU. The conference aimed to bring together a whole range of practitioners in the field of personalised education and to share ideas and practice from a whole range of sectors. More than just a handbook of the conference, the book aims to take the debate a stage further. The chapters are based on the conference addresses and workshops but the contributors have also responded to the debates and learning that took place at the gathering and written chapters especially intended for inclusion in this book.

Tony Jeffs gives a context and a history for personalised learning and shows that not only does it have a long and rich history but that at root, its values challenge the basis of the way governments perceive their relationship with civil society.

Peter Humphreys then shows that despite its claims to personalisation, the *modern* educational system is doing nothing more than customise what was already a very dilapidated and dysfunctional vehicle.

Following that, Alan Wilkins takes one of the central themes of personalised education, *co-operation* and shows how it can provide the basis for a mutual and democratic approach to learning. Then follows a series of case studies and practical examples of how personalised learning has been applied in a range of different settings.

Roland Meighan provides a case study of how learner-managed learning can work with group of learners in a teacher education setting. Lesley Saffran shows how the approach has been adopted successfully by home educating families in East London.

Ian Cunningham then demonstrates how the principles are put into practice with a group of young learners at the South Downs Learning Centre.

Jackie Rose rounds off this section by illustrating how the work of the *Bridge International Youth Project* in Stoke on Trent has used the principle of invitational, democratic learning as the basis for its work with marginalised and disadvantaged communities. The book rounds up, as the conference did, with a glimpse into the future with

Tim Rudd of Futurelab exploring some of the opportunities that new technologies offer us in developing personalized, learner-led learning.

What the conference achieved, and this book consolidates, is the recognition that personalised learning is not an abstract concept but a lively, vibrant, radical force being applied in a whole range of settings across the world. As an idea it has an illustrious past that presents solutions for the future. Though its contemporary practice provides a critique of existing education systems around the world, it does not focus its energies on providing solutions to the inherent problems of mass education. Instead, it practically addresses the needs of learners and shows how democratically organised, learner-lead learning, based on the principles of co-operation and willing participation provides the basis of a logical learning system fit for the 21st century.

Background

This book is the result of a partnership between The Creative Communitities Unit at Staffordshire University and the Centre for Personalised Education Trust.

Centre for Personalised Education Trust (CPE) is a charitable company whose trading name is *Personalised Education Now* (PEN). It promotes education based on learner-managed learning, using a flexible catalogue curriculum, located in a variety of settings, and operating within a framework of democratic values and practices. It is a membership organization publishing a Journal, Newsletters, E-briefings, and maintains a website,

www.c.person.ed.gn.apc.org

The *Creative Communities Unit* is based in the Faculty of Arts Media and Design at Staffordshire University is made up of a variety of staff with specialist skills in community arts, community development, community regeneration and youth work. It works across disciplinary boundaries and often works in partnership with other organisations. It undertakes a wide range of projects and offers accredited courses of varying lengths with flexible learning approaches and options, some delivered in the University and some in local communities.

www.staffs.ac.uk/ccu

Tel: 01782 294793

Acknowledgements

Thanks go to everyone who helped to organise the conference *Taking Choice Seriously* and who helped in the writing of this book. Special mention must go to Janet Meighan, Sarah Bonham, Barbara Emadi-Coffin, Mick Appleyard, Mike Gilsenan, Penny Vincent, Janet Hetherington.

Chapter one

Letting in the light

by Tony Jeffs

"Everything before us exists in the ideal world. The future is a blank and dreary void, like sleep or death, till the imagination brooding over it with wings outspread, impregnates it with life and motion. The forms and colours it assumes are but pictures reflected on the eye of fancy, the unreal mockeries of future events. The solid fabric of time and nature moves on, but the future always flies before it. "   William Hazlitt

Personalised education is an expression that only recently acquired a significant presence within the discourse of education. Although one would search with little expectation of success to encounter its use prior to the last two decades, as will be subsequently argued, the ideas, values and concepts it incorporates have a long and, in part, honourable history. Personalised education has both radical and conservative traits, as do say community education or home schooling. It would be naive to imagine otherwise. Although these two manifestations might, to borrow from Hazlitt, be unable to agree regarding 'the forms and colours' of a future society they do concur regarding what is the fundamental characteristic of personalised education; namely that it seeks to promote autonomous learner-managed education. To that end each advocate policies designed to encourage (even oblige) all to take responsibility for and control of their own learning pathways. Furthermore, each agree regarding certain inherent benefits that will flow from an expansion of personalised education in particular that, if pursued, it will bring about a transfer in the locus of power within education from teacher to student; and from institution to individual. On this much they see eye to eye, but on little else.

Conservatives and market liberals view personalised education in terms of possessive individualism. For them it translates into a mechanism whereby even greater competition can be incorporated into the world of education, promoting this not merely between institutions, in for example, the form of school league tables, but between individuals. By fostering autonomy and maximising the number of potential pathways open to an individual, they argue, all will be obligated to find a personal route, to engage in ceaseless competition to secure an advantage over others. Individuals will have to make choices, take risks and live by the obdurate rules of the market place. Marketisation will by this approach be inserted into every nook and cranny of the education system creating, so advocates believe, greater efficiency as it comes to replace a wasteful state monopoly with an 'educational' market obligated to respond to the choices and desires of the consumer or personalised learner. It is a system that aside from offering greater flexibility and responsiveness will, they assume, foster within the young the entrepreneurial skills essential for a prosperous economy. This model of personalised education draws its intellectual strengths from an individualistic view of society and an allegiance to the nineteenth century *laissez-faire* free market that advocated minimal state intervention.

Of course even during its hey-day the notion of the de-regulated market outside political and social control was a misnomer. For it was in part created and imperfectly sustained by often brutal state coercion, but that reality has been somewhat downplayed by those campaigning for market reforms who seek to prove that free markets promote and protect political democracy, a fraudulent claim unsupported by either history or contemporary experiences. The Thatcherite re-inventing of the free market and the imposition of policies by successive governments 'which make the market the only organising power in the economic sphere' (Polanyi 1944, 69) have led to the re-emergence of a market driven model of personalised education that had lain dormant for over a century.

However, it is not a model that has been uncontested. Not least because the failure of the free market to promote stability, social harmony and democracy remains as much a reality today as it did during the nineteenth century. Partly because there will always be more losers than winners, but also because, as in any market system, some, possibly most, suppliers will pursue short-term gains by making use of 'misleading' publicity. It is all very well intoning 'personalised educators beware' but how can an individual be confident the course offered in the prospectus or the schooling promised in the brochure matches the reality? The simple answer is that it cannot, and by the time they discover they have been misled it is usually too late.

In the United States during the last decade millions of dollar in fines have been imposed on universities for mis-selling courses (see Jeffs and Spence 2007). Whilst in the United Kingdom a growing body of evidence is accumulating that, even within the confines of our limited and partial market system, widespread cheating occurs amongst schools to secure higher league table rankings and exam results as well as better (than deserved) Ofsted reports. Likewise some universities and colleges are inflating marks and lowering standards to satisfy student demand for 'certification', and most are making exaggerated, if not downright dishonest, claims regarding not only the quality of their programmes but the relationship they have to career progression and life-time earnings. Finally, the attempt by the government to create a mass system of personalised learning via Individual Learning Accounts, the intention was to provide over a million of these annually, collapsed in 2002 after operating for only three years as a result of widespread fraud, abuse and incompetence amongst the 'for profit' providers of programmes (H of C Education and Skills Committee 2002a: 2002b). It was a near perfect example of how the greed of some providers, seeking short-term profit, undermines the legitimacy and survival of the market they rely upon. The cumulative result of all the recent attempts to link the personalisation and marketisation of education via the introduction of competitive markets is that rather than reducing the levels of bureaucracy and scale of state intervention, as intended, it has almost certainly achieved the opposite. A national curriculum, the intensification of the inspection system, the micro-management of many aspects of school and college life by circulars and conditions linked to funding streams, the ceaseless collection of data for the purposes of monitoring performance outcomes and the imposition of benchmarks, have all grown in tandem with every attempt to extend the writ of the market orientated model of personalised education.

Just as the market model of personalised education has a history so does, what might be called its communitarian or radical alternatives. However it is a discrete history. Paradoxically, the commun-itarian conceptualisations also shared a profound distrust of the state. This was not based upon a future-orientated fear that the state might at some upcoming date interfere to curtail the freedom of the market to protect the economically weak from exploitation but upon an understanding of how the state already worked to suppress dissent and defend the power of capital and patriarchy. Consequently amongst those most vocal in their promotion of mass education and democratic forms of governance during the early years of industrialisation were, for example the dissenting radical William Godwin; Mary Wollstonecraft the first writer to advocate women's and children's rights; Chartists such as William Lovett; and the co-operators following in the footsteps of Robert Owen who had established not only the first primary school but in all probability the first community and adult education centre; were also to found amongst the most determined opponents of state-managed education and articulate proponents of what would now be classified as personalised education. All feared state involvement would create a system focused on preparing young people for exploitation, that restricted their 'education' to what employers and the state deemed useful. Godwin believed, it would be impossible to administer without imposing on pupils *"the tyranny of implicit obedience. Go there; do that; write; rise; lie down; will perhaps for ever be the language addressed by youth by age"* (Godwin 1783: 23-4). Consequently they sought an alternative akin to that Wollstonecraft outlined in *A Vindication of the Rights of Women,* published in 1790,

> *"The most perfect education, in my opinion, is such an exercise of the understanding as is best calculated to strengthen the body and form the heart. Or, in other words, to enable the individual to attain such habits of virtue as well render it independent. In fact, it is a farce to call any being virtuous whose virtues do not result*

from the exercise of its own reason." (1975: 21)

In seeking an alternative to a state and employer controlled education system it was inevitable, given the paucity of contemporary or recent examples to draw upon, that radicals and reformers looked back to an Athenian past where democracy and learning had flourished. They rightly saw in the Socratic dialogues and informality of the Forum a prototypical example of what might be. A society where individuals might freely gather to engage in self-education and political debate; where *"power is in the hands not of a minority but of the whole people"* (Pericles quoted Thucydides 1972: 145).

The lesson learnt was that education, freedom and democracy flourish alongside each other and that none prosper for long without the support of the others. Moreover that all three require high levels of civic engagement and a sustained commitment amongst the citizenry to nourishing those threads that bind a community together, for the cultivation of what de Tocqueville (1839) was to call the 'habits of the heart' and Wollstonecraft 'the habits of virtue' that enabled individual liberty and collective democracy to fruitfully co-exist.

Simultaneously as they peered back to the Athenian world for inspiration, they gazed forward to a system of self-managed communal education. And in doing so they had promising exemplars to draw upon from more recent times. For example, the coffee-houses which had grown steadily in number from the 17th century onwards (Ellis 2004) and of which by 1700 there were over 2,000 in London and the provinces. Operating according to strict rules, which ensured orderly and democratic behaviour, they admitted all, irrespective of rank or wealth, who upon paying their penny were allotted to the first vacant seat on condition that they engaged in civil conversation and participated in any discussion already underway. Different coffee-houses acquired a reputation for specialising in topics such as politics, religion, science or literature (Kelly 1970).

As the century progressed these free 'universities' operated alongside an expanding array of debating societies, museums, music clubs, reading rooms and circulating libraries where self-organised education was provided by mutually supportive members. From 1780 these were augmented by Sunday Schools most initially linked to religious bodies but within a matter of decades many were being run by Chartists, Co-operaters and a heady mix of reformers and social activists. The first was opened by the flamboyant Robert Raikes in Gloucester, within a decade the inter-denominational Sunday School Society was claiming 250,000 members. Initially they were cross-generational welcoming people of all ages and besides providing educational classes and libraries most also served as 'welfare agencies' running saving clubs, clothing banks and the like. The crucial point was that this rich array of autonomous educational and social provision was successful in educational terms.

Certainly it is possible to argue that the literacy levels achieved by this mix of self-help, philanthropy, Dame Schools and, after 1832, minimalist state funding for religious schools, was by 1870 were remarkably high. Comparative analysis of literacy levels over long periods of time is an imperfect science but they probably accomplished rates not far short of that reached by our nurseries, schools and colleges after eleven years of compulsory attendance (see for example Rose 2002; also Shannon 1990). Crucially these Institutes, Reading Rooms and Adult Schools, so often founded upon principles of voluntary attendance and co-operation, did much to foster a democratic spirit and love of lifetime learning. Rose in his magisterial study of working-class education cites numerous examples of how they achieved this. One account by William Farish a handloom weaver living in Carlisle, written around 1840, will suffice:

> "Hiring a six-loom weaving shop in Blue Anchor Lane, we fitted it up ourselves with desk and seats, rude enough, doubtless, but we could not very well complain of our own handiwork, and there was nobody else to please. The [Carlisle] Mechanics' Institution, although well managed and liberally supported, had failed somewhat in its mission, mainly, as we thought, through the reluctance of the weaver in his clogs and fustian jacket to meet in the same room with the better clad, and possibly better mannered, shop assistants and clerks of the city. So these new places were made purely democratic, having no master, and not permitting even any in the management but such as lived by weekly wages. Those who could read taught those who could not, and those who could cipher did the same for those less advanced". (quoted Rose 2001:64)

We also learn from the same source that in Carlisle during the this period there were at least 24 reading rooms with a membership of 1,400, which meant around a fifth of the adult population were affiliated to one or another.

For all their poverty and squalor the new industrial towns and cities were educationally rich in terms of self-managed and communal resources. The array of facilities enabled those who wished to do so to control their own education and to find enrichment via both individual and collective study. The vitality of this provision, unlike the grim visage of the towns themselves, impressed Niklaj Grundtvig, the

Danish social reformer, educationalist and theologian, during his study visits to Britain. He returned determined to create an educational structure independent of the state, akin to that advocated by Lovett and the Chartists, but funded, in the interests of social justice, by progressive general taxation. Lovett failed, but against all the odds Grundtvig and his allies succeeded. The result was the network of Scandinavian Folk High Schools, free schools and study circles that provide a unique example of state-funded personalised education that still flourish today. Collectively they, along with the high quality of cultural provision also found in those countries, comprise perhaps the only system that allows for an individual to fashion across a lifetime a personalised educational 'journey' within a state funded system.

In Britain a highly centralised system of compulsory schooling gradually, but ruthlessly, eradicated any alternatives that posed a serious threat to its hegemony. A few fringe, usually privately funded initiatives, lingered but until recently little space was allowed for personalised education or progressive alternatives. Even the right to home-based education had to be fought for over many years. Adult education has been gradually incorporated into a system devoted to narrowly focused training for employment until little now remains of the rich network of university and local authority liberal education that once flourished. After over a century of increasingly intensive state involvement in schooling and adult education we have acquired, much as Godwin and the others predicted, a restricted 'productivist' model of education. But as we shall see this attempt to subordinate education to training has produced a healthy reaction in recent years.

Pulling in different directions

With regards to educational techniques and modes of practice it is advantageous to recognise that these are of themselves overwhelmingly neutral. What counts is how they are employed, for all educational interventions can either seek to liberate or subordinate the student. Personalised education is no exception to this general rule, possessing both reactionary and radical, negative and positive antecedents and applications. For example in relation to the former a substantial number of parents in the past opted to 'privatise' and 'personalise' their children's education to prevent any mixing with those from 'inferior' families. In particular the wealthy, living in rural areas or abroad, especially prior to the appearance of accessible affordable high status private boarding schools, frequently employed governesses and tutors to avoid the risk of 'contamination'. Nowadays this is almost unknown in Britain as parents anxious to isolate their children from those perceived as socially or racially 'inferior' do so by moving to up-market neighbourhoods or paying for private schooling.

However, the urge to isolate and inhibit remains but now it tends to be driven by different motives. In particular the education of some children is 'privatised' and 'personalised' in order to restrict its content and control social contact. In the United States and elsewhere religious fundamentalists, in particular, see 'personalised' home schooling as an effective way of minimising the contamination of their children by ideas and ways of reading the world that they, as adults, find unpalatable, and as a means to reduce the possibility their off-spring will acquire the sort of inquisitive questioning mind that might encourage them to in turn challenge and interrogate their parents' religious or social beliefs. In relation to further and higher education we can see a parallel use of 'personalised education' as an inhibitor. Here employers increasingly manufacture individualised training programmes designed to ensure what is taught is purely 'practical' and focused on their needs not those of the employee. Stripped of theory such self-contained programmes curb the capacity of employees to challenge the authority of management and by being delivered at home or in the workplace deny participants the chance to engage with those studying other subjects at places of general education. Such employer-led personalised training or learning, for example NVQs, unlike earlier models of apprenticeship, are denuded of any 'liberal educational' content for they seek to close down rather than open-up the educational horizons of participants.

In this and other respects what we are encountering is something different from personalised education, a discrete variation – personalised learning. All too often these two are perceived as inter-changeable, two sides of the same coin. This is not the case. Learning is an activity and process that takes place in diverse settings and contexts. It may be part of an educational experience leading to understanding and autonomy. However, it may also be a mechanistic encounter or part of a process of indoctrination, for example the rote learning of health and safety regulations or how to pluck chickens. Dogs learn tricks, people learn to ride a bike, and in this sense learning implies a more limited aim. Many things that children and adults learn, formally and informally, cannot be regarded as contributing to their education. For education implies a much richer experience than the mere activity of learning. As Peters explains education, unlike learning, training or indoctrination, to be taking place three criteria have to be met. These are:

> "That 'education' implies the transmission of what is worth-while to those who become committed to it;
> That 'education' must involve knowledge and understanding and some kind of cognitive perspective, which are not inert;
> That 'education' at least rules out some procedures of transmission, on the grounds that they lack wittingness and voluntariness."
>
> (1966: 45)

One may contest elements of this analysis (see for example Langford 1973) but even critics concede that learning and education are not synonymous. Certainly in relation to personalised education it is essential within the current policy context for advocates of the former to distinguish between the two. Indeed the survival of personalised education, as a discrete activity, may well depend upon a readiness to do so. Education policy has a history of incorporating and reordering what were distinctive forms of practice so that the title remains but what is undertaken in its name bears little relationship to what went before. In recent years community schooling, youth work and community education have each been denuded of their historic meaning and the labels applied to radically different forms of practice. It is not just that personalised learning is significantly different from personalised education but that any failure to acknowledge this may well lead to the latter being subsumed within the former.

Paradoxically whilst one constituency personalises education in order to better indoctrinate and micro-manage the lives of their children others, with equal enthusiasm, embrace it to enable their off-spring to avoid the indoctrination and micro-management of the school system. One of the most under-reported but significant educational developments of the last two decades has been the growth in Britain and the United States of the home school movement. What makes this trend so important is that it is the first sustained challenge to the unbridled expansion of state controlled education for over a century. Mass compulsory education has existed for less than a century and a half in Britain and in most countries for an even shorter period. Apart from a brief period during the 1914-18 war it has grown in scope and scale without serious hindrance. That growth has taken a number of forms.

First the length of compulsory schooling has been elongated both by the raising of the school-leaving age, soon to be 18, and a lowering of the age of initial entry. Second we have witnessed a gradual bloating of the school-day. Extended schooling has meant young people starting earlier, for some as early 07.30, and finishing as late as 18.00. Lunchtimes have been re-configured, in part as a result of government intervention, to prevent young people leaving the school premises during the day without the express permission of their parents. And likewise playtimes have overwhelmingly been condensed, and even eliminated. Four traditional school-holidays have been curtailed with young people increasingly corralled into organised and monitored play schemes, often school-based, and specialist classes for the 'gifted and talented' or 'remedial'. Finally compulsory homework has been extended, despite serious doubts being raised as to its value, thereby reducing the free time allotted young people outside of school hours.

Few of these changes can be justified on educational grounds. Virtually all are designed to enable parents to work longer and or more flexible hours and to control the leisure time of young people by removing them from public spaces. Inevitably fatigue and boredom take their toll, fuelling disruption in the classroom, absenteeism and conflict and bullying. The rise of personalised education is in part a reaction against these developments. But is also driven by other changes occurring within the state system:

- The growth in the size of the institutions. For in order to expand the hours and length of schooling without proportionately pushing up costs it has been essential for schools, state and private, to achieve economies of scale by growing ever larger. This has unquestionably contributed to the alienation of both teachers and pupils and led to introduction of the intensive electronic surveillance of young people. Expansion in size has also resulted in a significant weakening of school-community ties as the size of the catchment areas grow.

- The imposition of a national curriculum upon state pupils and the regimentation of learning required to deliver that curriculum and secure the outcomes linked to it has resulted in the alienation of many pupils and parents. State schools can no longer even try to offer a rounded or negotiated curriculum.

- The increasing emphasis on socialisation rather than education within the school syllabus. Schools have always attended to the moral, physical and social wellbeing of the young people who attend them, but this was a subsidiary role. However what has occurred in recent years is that governments have viewed schools as either a prime or major means of shaping the behaviour of the general public. For instance social problems as diverse as crime, obesity, family failure, mental illness, sexual health, drug abuse the political alienation and religious extremism been tackled by tinkering with the curriculum or social milieu of schools. Consequently in the state sector the educational role has been devalued as the emphasis on socialisation has grown. More recently following the Laming Report education departments have been integrated into Children Services Departments or Trusts dominated by a protectionist agenda that requires schools to monitor children and collect extensive data on their lives within school and beyond.

- This results in the growing use of schools as warehouses both to contain young people to allow their parents to work but also to solve the problem of youth unemployment. Paradoxically as young people have been denied entry into the adult world of work so schools have been obliged to artificially replicate it within their own borders. At an ever-younger age they are expected to 'opt' for career route, at the expense of their general education even though they may not actually enter employment for a decade or more after that choice is made. Exclusion from the real world of work means schools and colleges are required to socialise them beforehand. The result is that secondary schools, and universities, less and less perceive their role in terms of offering an education, but as places set aside to prepare pupils for employment.

These and other factors have each helped to stimulate a growth in home-based education and other forms of personalised education. Individuals and self-governing groups have sought 'human-scale' alternatives both to the statutory school system and an adult 'education' structure that focuses exclusively on training, employability and skills. The result has been a gradual emergence of alternatives such as small independent schools, groups of parents coming together in home-based education co-operatives and an expansion in, for example, reading circles, local and family history groups, web-based adult education and autonomous provision such as the University of the Third Age. It would be mistaken to classify these as merely re-active for they have also been encouraged by a realisation that the inter-net and other forms of electronic knowledge make it both feasible and advantageous to step outside of a school and college system rooted in and wedded to a Fordist mass-production model of education. This coupled to a creeping awareness of the gross inefficiency of the schools and colleges - where hours are wasted on institutional management; overseeing students; socialising the 'anti-social'; servicing the internal and external bureaucracy; and preparing for and taking tests – encourages individuals and collectives to seek out alternatives such as personalised education. Alternatives that promise so much more for all concerned in terms of self-fulfilment, wellbeing and opportunities for educational progression.

Self-evidently the enormous investment, physical and emotional, in schools and other institutions will continue to impede the growth of all forms of personalised education. And not simply because they consume so much in terms of resources and goodwill that could be more profitably spent on those things that go towards creating an educationally and culturally rich society. Now, as in the past, politicians, bureaucrats and employers will not willing surrender the power they possess to manage and control the education of others. Neither will the highly paid leaders who do their bidding at the institutional level work to dismantle a system that rewards them well for managing it. Eventually escalating costs and diminishing returns will probably press root and branch reform onto the agenda but when that occurs, like the outcome, it is impossible to predict. In the meantime various forms of personalised education will certainly prosper on the margins but progress will remain slow. What probably threatens growth the most is not the existing institutions lacking as they do the self-belief in and enthusiasm for what they are doing to mount a serious challenge. Rather it is the well documented falling away in civic engagement (see for example Putman 2000; Skocpol, 2003; Sennett 1998, 2006). This poses a serious challenge for two, inter-related, reasons; first it threatens the survival of the myriad voluntary and local government funded organisations and agencies that enable personalised education to flourish. The sports clubs, youth groups, libraries, cultural groups, social movements, leisure clubs and so on that provide the warp and weft of associational life, these are crucial for all forms of personalised education as they enable individuals to move beyond self and engage in collective education.

There are things that cannot be learnt or understood in isolation. It is no accident home educated young people as adults are far more likely to join clubs and associations and to volunteer (Webb 1999). Having been gifted the opportunity to join on a voluntary basis ands spared the forced collectivisation of schooling they are far more likely to acquire an appreciation of the value of civic engagement and associational life. The irony is that individualism flourishes within mass institutions and organisations. For they actively foster competition both by dividing and ruling staff and students in order to better control and manage them and in order to 'motivate' both to undertake routinised tasks and learn for, and teach to, tests. By way of contrast it is the survival of personalised education and human-scale organisations that are placed in jeopardy by the expansion and intensification of individualism. Second the erosion of civic engagement and civil society alongside a growth in 'contracting out' of participation in social action to professionals (Maloney 1999; Skocpol 2003) makes it extremely difficult to create the sort of educationally rich society that will kindle and promote personalised education.

The demand for education is not fixed, although it may be difficult to measure, some societies value it more than others, much as some individuals prioritise more than their neighbours. For all the glib talk of a 'learning society' and 'lifelong learning' it would be difficult to argue that our society has become more educationally rich during the last few decades. The process of 'dumbing down' is almost certainly not as acute as writers like Bywater (2006) and Law (2006) suggest but it is the case that few university towns outside of Oxford and Cambridge, let alone other centres of population, now support a serious well-stocked bookshop, a repertory theatre or art-house cinema. Of course these facilities are not the sole indicators of an educationally rich environment, one might for instance add parks, museums, community centres, pubs where conversation can occur, libraries and public art, but without them it is difficult to talk of a culturally endowed community that encourages and supports the efforts of individuals and groups to take control of their own education and cultural development.

Conclusion

Historically personalised education has never been a simplistically individualistic system. It is one that can only flourish when all work towards the creation of self-regulating communities that value education and provide abundant opportunities for individuals and groups to learn together and from each other. It is an open system. It, therefore, can ultimately only thrive in an open society. Personalised education, as a consequence, cannot ultimately co-exist for long with autocracy, imposed hierarchies, theocratic domination or bureaucratic control for it is founded upon a belief that individuals and groups can pursue knowledge and wisdom in their own ways, and may question and query, challenge and probe as and when they see fit. Thereby it simultaneously nourishes and feeds off those democratic structures that permit individuals to engage in free open dialogue and form and affiliate to communities of enquiry as and when they choose. Freedom of thought, freedom of movement and freedom of assembly are essential for the long-term survival of an environment within which personalised education is able to flourish. As Dewey reminds us this

"Freedom of thought denotes freedom of thinking; specific doubting, inquiring, suspense, creating and cultivating of tentative hypotheses, trials or experimenting that are unguaranteed and that involve risks of waste, loss and error." (1958: 222)

Personalised education, indeed any educational model wedded to the nurturing of freedom of thought, will therefore invariably challenge the assumptions and desires of those who may seek to control and limit what others learn. As Dewey implies, in the short-term this may seem profligate in terms of resources, after all individuals might choose to learn things that do not produce self-evident outcomes related to the promotion of economic growth. Equally it may kindle social dissonance by encouraging debate and doubt rather than superficial cohesion and uniformity. For those who have faith in the power of education to transform individuals and societies for the better, these are risks well worth taking. Indeed they are frequently precursors of progress. After all there is nothing inherently radical regarding personalised education. However, because it seeks to release individuals and groups from the dead hand of tradition and offers all the opportunity to follow what Grundtvig (Koch 1952) christened the 'winged word' it holds out real promise and like Hazlitt's future 'flies before' in hope and expectation. First, because the focus is on the need for each of us to take responsibility for our own education thereby encouraging an independence of mind as well as a commitment to the social world that provides collective opportunities for learning. Second, because it fosters dialogue and active learning rather passivity. In both these respects it has clear linkages with a Socratic tradition that holds the 'unexamined life is not worth living' and Hazlitt's optimistic 'pictures of reflected on the eye of fancy'.

Bibliography

Bywater, M. (2006) *Big Babies*: *Or why can't we just grow up?* London: Granta

De Tocqueville (1839) *Democracy in America*, (reprinted 1969) New York: Harper.

Dewey, J. (1958) *Experience and Nature*, New York: Dover.

Ellis, M. (2004) *The Coffee House: A cultural history*, London: Weidenfeld and Nicolson.

House of Commons Education and Skills Committee (2002a) *Individual Learning Accounts: Third Report of Session 2001-02 (Volume 1)*, London: HMSO Stationary Office.

House of Commons Education and Skills Committee (2002b) *Individual Learning Accounts: Third Report of Session 2001-02 (Volume 2)*, London: HMSO Stationary Office.

Jeffs, T. and Spence (2008) 'Farewell to all that? The uncertain future of youth and community work training' in *Youth and Policy (98)*.

Kelly, T. (1970) *A History of Adult Education in Great Britain*, Liverpool: Liverpool University Press.

Koch, H. (1952) *Grundtvig*, Yellow Springs, Ohio: Antioch Press.

Langford, G. (1973) 'The Concept of Education' in G. Langford and D. J. O'Connor (eds.) *New Essays in the Philosophy of Education*, London: Routledge, Kegan and Paul.

Law, S. (2006) *The War for Children's Minds*, London: Routledge.

Maloney, W. (1999) 'Contracting out the Participation Function: social capital and cheque-book participation' in J. W. van Deth, M. Maraffi, K. Newton and P.E. Whiteley (eds.) *Social Capital and European Democracy*, London: Routledge.

Peters, R. S. (1966) *Ethics and Education*, London: Unwin.

Polanyi, K. (1944) *The Great Transformation: The political and economic origins of our time*, Boston: Beacon Press.

Putman, R. (2000) *Bowling Alone: The collapse and revival of American community*, New York: Simon and Schuster.

Rose, J. (2002) *The Intellectual Life of the British Working Classes*, Cambridge, Mass.: Yale Nota Bene.

Skocpol, T. (2003) *Diminished Democracy. From membership to management in American civic life*, Norman, Oklahoma: University of Oklahoma Press.

Sennett, R. (1998) *The Corrosion of Character: The personal consequences of work in the new capitalism*, New York: Norton.

Sennet, R. (2006) *The Culture of the New Capitalism*, Cambridge, Mass.: Yale University Press.

Shannon, P. (1990) 'The Struggle to Continue: Progressive Reading Instruction in the United States', Portsmouth, NH: Heinemann.
Thucydides (1972 *The Peloponnesian War*, Harmondsworth: Penguin.

Webb, J. (1999) *Those Unschooled Minds: Home-educated children grow up*, Nottingham: Educational Heretics Press.

Wollstonecraft, M. (1975) *A Vindication of the Rights of Woman*, New York: Norton.

Chapter two

Personalised Education: A Framework for Evaluation and Educational Reconstruction.

by Peter Humphreys

Chapter synopsis

Eight principles are explored along dimensions describing shallow to deep levels of personalisation. These underpinning principles can be used as a framework enabling evaluation of the degree of personalisation in any educational experience, or setting. They are as useful for the learner, teacher, and mentor as they are for the thought leaders, strategists and politicians thinking about the future of education and society. They describe the agenda for personalisation, choice and the transformation of our learning systems. The chapter moves on to examine some implications for the development of a personalised learning system.

Introduction

Although comfortingly familiar, I propose that the current educational paradigm has run its course. Schooling in particular fails to meet its stated educational and societal goals and its culture has inflicted a suffocating malaise across education and our outlook on life itself. Personalisation as discussed in this chapter is premised on *taking choice seriously*. This *deep and transformative personalisation* goes beyond the customised and tailored scenarios emerging in current thinking *(Gilbert et al, 2006)*. These are best described as '*mass customisation*' or '*shallow personalisation*' *(Leadbeater, 2006)*. *Deep personalisation* moves to *self-creation - authentic self-managed learning, co-created with others on an invitational basis from a "personalised educational landscape" (Humphreys, 2004)*. It is a view that begins to develop a unifying vision of how we integrate learning and living, and the shift we need to make in the 21st century towards personal responsibility, participatory democracy, sustainable values, entrepreneurial activity, community cohesion and life-long learning.

Existing learning systems are characterised by their *one-size-fits-all* approach underpinned by a deficit view of young people. They remain resistant to personalisation because their inflexible, imposed structures and organisation mitigate against it, and present significant barriers to life and social cohesion.

The schooling system epitomises the complete lack of imagination brought to bear on the issue and was exemplified as long ago as 1911 by Edmond Holmes whilst Chief Inspector of Schools:

> *"In nine schools out of ten, on nine days out of ten, in nine lessons out of ten, the teacher is engaged in laying thin films of information on the surface of the child's mind and then after a brief interval he (or she) is skimming these off to satisfy him/herself that the information has been duly laid … Conscription-based schooling and uniform curriculum imposed by adults on children is an affront to learning."*
> *Edmond Holmes, 1911*

A century later little has changed.

The existing, educational landscape variations should be acknowledged:

"Playgroups, nursery, early excellence centres, KS1(infants), KS2 (juniors), KS3 & 4 (secondary school), further and higher education colleges, traditional universities, Open University, University of the First Age, University of the Third Age, early childhood 'natural learning' at home, home-based education, Cubs, Scouts, Brownies, Guides, Boys Brigade, Woodcraft Folk, Duke of Edinburgh Award Scheme, Public Library, Learning clubs for sports and the arts, book-circles, learning co-operatives, community learning centres, apprenticeships, work training and educational programmes, workers educational associations, adult education programmes, voluntary and support programmes, gap years, career breaks, activity holiday programmes, fundamentalist religious school, driving school, community arts programmes, science / museum / environmental centres, personal tuition etc There are schools varying from the Danish EFTA residential model, to the City as School 'school without walls' approach, to the Summerhill democratic version, to that of the radical Sudbury Valley School, USA, to Canadian Cyber-schools, to Virtual Schools to Flexi-colleges etc." (Meighan, 2005)

The reader will be able to add to this list and recognise that some learning settings and experiences retain elevated status whilst others are marginalised. The landscape is dominated by mainstream routes. Attracting massive funding they are guardians of the preferred pathways and so called gold standards. But is this really deserved and is it whole story? The real outcomes of education are surely to be found in the richness of lives and contributions of our citizens within a peaceful and sustainable society. Few would argue that real problems do not remain here. The evidence for those who take more personalised routes is that whatever their background they rise to the flexibilities and responsibilities afforded to them. They gain much from their wider experiences, enjoy happier and more productive lives.

The exploration of what personalisation means, what a *personalised educational landscape* could comprise and how it could work, benefits from looking broadly at learning and educational options. Settings and experiences currently at the margins are an invaluable illustration of the key principles.

Principles of personalisation

The approach taken here unpacks the very DNA, the building blocks of a personalised learning system rather than looking for a finished blueprint as systems have done up until this point. Understanding personalisation principles and the degree of personalisation provides a framework for evaluation and indicators for the development of a continuously adaptive *personalised educational landscape.*

The eight principles that follow are drawn from a rich, but largely untapped vein of theory, practice and evidence. They are aligned with and go beyond the societal outcomes governments so often profess but fail to achieve. Space precludes a full discussion here but essentially they underpin personalisation in any educational setting or experience.

1. Degree of LEARNER CONTROL:
Personalisation needs learner–managed and co-constructed learning - to meet learning

styles and preferences and supported by a range of others.

Key rationale:

•   Evidence, from brain science, child development, from practice and observation reveals that choice, ownership and responsibility are keys to engagement, motivation and deep learning.

•   We are essentially social learners and will request a variety of support, monitoring, challenge and review. This can be facilitated by a range of professional educators and co-learners.

•   Learners who lead, manage and co-create their own learning draw upon a wider educational landscape, are able to choose and challenge their own preferred learning styles and in doing so develop their own *learning and teaching repertoire*. In turn this is shared with others and develops a cumulative resource within the family, community and society as a whole.

2 Degree of LEARNER DEPENDENCY:

Personalisation needs a shift from dependency to independence and interdependency - based on the principals of *subsidiarity*, personal responsibility and choice.

Key rationale:

•   Our dominant learning systems generate dependency and are counter-productive for a sustainable, adaptive, innovative and mature 21st century democracy.

•   Dependency is disabling and damaging to self-development and maturity.

•   Dependency unnecessarily exacerbates generational issues and ageism.

•   The principle of *subsidiarity* determines those who are capable enough take responsibility for their learning and life regardless of any other factor like age, sex, race or disability.

- Living and working more interdependently is an advantage for family, societal and global sustainability and social cohesion.

3.   Degree of LEARNER CHOICE:
Personalisation needs invitational learning and assessment – within institutions, contexts, settings and experiences
Key rationale:
- Choice, ownership and responsibility are keys to engagement, motivation and deep learning. This cannot continue in a learning landscape where schooling has an effective monopoly with its coercive culture.
- *Invitational* learning is learner-driven, responsive, flexible and adaptive.
- *Invitational* learning is financially effective and efficient. It does not incur the massive *fall out* costs used to massage the casualties of schooling. Neither is it burdened with the expenditure associated with those who later become disengaged from their families and communities evidenced in crime, anti-social behaviours, poor physical and mental health.

4.   Degree of 'EDVERSITY' (educational diversity): Personalisation involves learning from a varied educational landscape of opportunities - within physical and virtual places and spaces
Key rationale:
- There is currently limited recognition or use of the wider educational landscape, as outlined below, and the massive formal / informal / professional / community learning resource (physical and virtual).
- We need to acknowledge, legitimise, support, fund and access a *personalised educational landscape.* It would include all learning resources: human and physical,

institutional and virtual to be found in current educational sectors, in homes, libraries, workplaces, community arts and adult learning programmes, our science and art museums, television and public services and individual learners. It is an abundant, e-enabled, life-long learning landscape of which our current institutions become just one transformed part.

• Educational diversity – *edversity* *(Humphreys, 2004a)* goes beyond silo, containerised and linear thinking, responding more flexibly and in an adaptive way to learner and societal needs.

• *Edversity* protects against the stifling effects of current monoculture models.

5. Degree of INTEGRATION: Personalisation needs re-integration of learning, life and community - because life is not necessarily lived to a pre-determined linear pattern. This implies interweaving learning with all aspects of living and community.

Key rationale:

• Lives, education and learning have been scripted into a restricted idea called schooling.

• Institutions are organised around outdated notions of childcare, linear patterns of life, work and careers.

• Family and generational cohesion are threatened by the separation created by age-stage schooling.

• Creative, flexible and sustainable non-linear patterns of living are largely prevented by our schooling systems.

• There is limited recognition and use of the massive community learning resource. The opportunity to develop family, community and societal *learning capital* is lost.

• Learning and social cohesion could be extended through authentic action and community-based issues education.

• Schooling organisation adversely impacts on the environment and commercial life, amplifying aspects like travel congestion and pollution peaks, skews and constrains business, leisure and holiday patterns.

6. Degree of DEMOCRACY:

Personalisation requires democratic values, organization and practice - since democracy is not pre-determined it has to be cultivated and developed.

Key rationale:

• Currently, lip service is paid to democracy. Much of what we have is uniformed, fragmentary and tokenistic.

• To value and sustain democracy requires continuous cultivation.

• Democratic values and organisation need to be practiced in our daily lives.

• Guidance to these values already exists in UN Rights and Responsibilities.

• Needs, rights and responsibilities of all need to be acknowledged.

• Young people are capable of reasoned argument and understanding, and behaving democratically.

• The *fall-out and* casualties of limited democracy threaten its existence. A cohort of disengaged citizens runs the risk of being replaced with totalitarian regimes.

• Lack of democracy strikes at family, societal and global sustainability and cohesion.

7.Degree of CURRICULUM CONTROL:

Personalisation requires the catalogue and natural versions of curriculum and assessment – imposition needs to be replaced by choice from pre-existing curriculum catalogues thus developing the learner's own natural preferences.

Key rationale:

• Currently schooling is an uninvited, pre-determined, pre-packaged curriculum and assessment system, breeding disengagement and superficial learning.

• We develop over-schooled and mis-educated people.

• Many accreditations assume value beyond their actual worth.

• Too little learning originates from the learner and their choices, desires and dispositions.

• All sorts of curriculum are needed - pre-packaged, bespoke and natural, catering for differing needs in a learner's journey. All can be part of an invitational catalogue curriculum.

• Society needs engaged, motivated life-long learners and cannot afford disengagement and shallow learning.

8. Degree of AGE LINKAGE: Personalisation requires the de–coupling of age–stage progressions and assessments - with learner-managed learning as the principle of life-long education.

Key rationale:

• The brain-based, practical evidence for age–stage is not convincing.

• Age-stage thinking and ageism are perpetuated by schooling. They fail to meet the needs of learners.

• Age-stage thinking favours *one-size-fits-all* solutions. It produces minimal competency and massive underachievement. It supports dubious notions of success and failure whilst fuelling the *special needs industry.*

- Age-stage thinking infects both educators and learners, inhibits learning and creates institutional barriers.
- Age-stage thinking develops a target culture, fuelling disengagement from real learning.
- Age-stage thinking assumes we can capture all learning in pre-determined, pre-packaged curricula and imposed assessment - it is inherently inflexible and continuously outdated
- Age-stage thinking develops an ageist approach to living and weakens social cohesion.
- *Learner-managed learning* is a better guide, representing motivation and commitment as much as it does notions of current capacity and future potential.

(Based on Humphreys, 2004b and 2007)

Personalised Education: a Framework for Evaluation

What we have here is one way of exploring the anatomy of personalisation and choice. The principles support a dialogue and signpost educational futures. The simplified diagram Fig.1 *Personalised Education: Framework for Evaluation (Humphreys, 2005)* hints at how these indices can be used as multi-purpose evaluation tools. The degree of personalisation in any learning experience or setting can be identified using the horizontal maturity dimension for each principle.

In a more developed form, where settings or experiences are located in the framework, anyone can get a comparative understanding of where each stands in relation to others. The tool can then support learner voice and choice, enabling preferences to be established and followed. Additionally, if exemplars are built into the tool anybody can use the framework to self-evaluate against personalisation criteria and continuously review and develop practice.

The framework illustrates very clearly that there is a **personalisation continuum**. Simplistic, stereotypical classifications made of mainstream or alternative settings are insufficient. The continuum allows deeper analysis.

Complex interpretations can arise but essentially learning systems that operate wholly or mainly to the left of the continuum are predominantly inflexible. At times and for various reasons a rigid learning setting or experience may be chosen. Any organisation or group which works on compulsion and prescription such as mainstream schools or an alternative institution or a rigid home-based education regime, have from the outset severely limited any notion of personalisation.

Implications for a *Personalised Educational Landscape*

Meighan (2005) offered ten suggestions that signpost a personalised landscape and the future re-orientation of institutions like schools. They reflect some established and promising settings and ideas. He included the following each with a rationale:

1. *Year-Round Education (YRE)*
2. *Flexischooling*
3. *Home-based Education*
4. *Home-based learning education co-operatives*
5. *Community Arts programmes*
6. *The Public Library*
7. *NotschoolNet*
8. *Citischool*
9. *Efterskole*
10. *Village College or Local Community Learning Centres*

Meighan then gives examples of possible *"journeys and episodes"* and compared them with the uninspiring, pre-packaged 3-19 schooling experience on offer to most. Learning in a personalised landscape could be undertaken for *any agreed periods of time, at any age and in any combination.* Pressure to meet age-stage norms, study particular age related material or to enter different sectors is removed. *Readiness* and guided choice become the drivers.

Existing resource-rich schools would become just one recycled part of this *edversity.* Clearly this would require substantial attitudinal and cultural shifts. *Edversity* is not about institutional inertia, passive learners and inflexible offers. It is about vibrant learning networks, choice and student voice *(see Rudd, Colligan, Naik 2006 and Meighan, 2005).* It does not require learners to *power down* technologically nor does it abdicate itself to imposed *school learning.* It is established on open access to the richness of the learning landscape beyond. The best and most useful of the current curricula may continue to be used by choice, but personal need would drive more *issue-based and integrated learning from the catalogue curriculum.*

Learners become *travellers* controlling their own learning and life with *continuous options. They can learn independently, in groups, take up packaged learning or bespoke learning journeys.* Learners can investigate a range of *learning pathways, co-constructing their personal learning plans* with the assistance of a new teaching profession of *learning travel agents and guides, along with members of families and people in the community.* These are the *new* educationalists that broker and accommodate groups of learners and help with research and advice where learning skills are required.

Qualified learning travel agents and intelligent ICT (information communications technology) agencies would offer *information, reflection, and challenge, and a 24/7/365 network of invitational support* as the basis for deep learning, engagement and motivation.

The potential of ICT and DT (digital technologies) is developing rapidly. They make the personalised landscape approach even more persuasive and a practical reality. Whilst not replacing human contact they can extend opportunity and choice by *connecting, energising and facilitating the landscape.* They shape new *learning environments, pedagogies, tools and media for learning.* Learners are assisted to learn at their *preferred time and pace, anytime and anywhere.* The technologies support e-assessment, mentoring, coaching and continuous feedback. ICT and DT become a part of the *learner's toolkit and media, the learner's communication and evidence base.*

Institutions would remain by aligning with personalisation principles but now **convivial rather coercive**. Current work, life and care patterns would probably mean that at the outset most young people would continue to learn in *recycled institutions*. With time, it is likely that learners would become more adventurous and explore the potential of other learning-life journeys and episodes on the basis of seeing what these flexibilities permit and achieve. There would then be a move away from dependency to independence and interdependency models. Evidence from existing examples of learner-managed learning suggest that the majority of learners would make this transition extremely successfully whilst recognising that, personal needs will require different degrees and types of support.

Implications for the schooling system

Schools as we know them could not exist as personalised settings in anything other than the most superficial sense. However, they can be recycled *(see Humphreys, P (edit) 2007.*

Given that schools remain the key institution covering the geographical and human landscape they are ideally situated to become the bases, places and spaces for a range of learning settings and activities. I believe their real benefit to a *personalised educational landscape* would be to emerge as world class *invitational, all-age local community learning centres (CLC)*.

Imagine what this could mean by 2025:

Schools have now evolved into all-age Community Learning Centres (CLC) open 24/7 and all the year round. They have outstanding world-class facilities for learning, sport and leisure, housed in buildings of inspirational design, flexibility and functionality. Typically, they are built around a comprehensive multi-media library, ICT hub and resource centre. Here much of the community media and publishing facilities are based. Cultural, sporting, health and social service components exist according to local needs and there are extensive childcare facilities for all ages permitting access to the new flexibilities available in the landscape.

CLC networks are bases for the pedagogues (PEDAs) (see Meighan 2005) and extended educational professionals - master educators steeped in the knowledge and skills of how we learn, how we can accelerate learning, and in human development. They act in many roles: guides, mentors, coaches, tutors, teachers and assessors. They assist in co-producing personal learning plans and help in solution building. They

bring together learners with learning experiences and courses. They put learners in touch with key professionals in CLCs; with community-based tutors and volunteers; with work experiences and apprenticeships. They are important guides and links beyond the local community. They help co-create learning journeys, inspire and challenge.

Learning takes place in a range of settings in the landscape according to the needs, aspirations and aptitudes of the learner. CLCs still run curricular courses but rarely in groups of more than 10. This facilitates the high quality and quantity of discourse expected. The CLCs operate on various cycles so that not all learners and staff and others are in at the same time. There are no traditional schooldays, weekends and holidays – maximum choice and fluidity of organisational arrangements is made.

Distance learning is widely available with external expertise being channelled in via digital links and local follow up. Most learners have flexible learning paths and plans with episodes made up of localised CLC activities, independent study, travel and residential experiences, distance learning and small group tutoring whist others have periods of home learning. They follow a mixture of their own naturally defined curricula and they select and modify the catalogue of curricula found locally and globally.

Experiences are open to all regardless of age. Independence and interdependence are gained and developed from the early years. Highly committed learners learn more and more effectively than they did under mass-schooling; they are motivated and driven, not coerced and dragged. They are freed from enforced timescales, lessons, terms and years. Readiness is pivotal.

Learning is contextualised in communities where it is valued highly and responsibility is shared. Learning is available anytime and independent of place. All citizens have access to the latest ICT, worldwide web and digital connections at home. The country long considered this digital investment as a prerequisite in a modern educational landscape and is recognised as a freely available utility.

(Based on Humphreys, 2004a)

How do we move on?

Such a transformation requires an evolutionary approach occurring concurrently with commitment and capacity to build and sustain it. This truly values diversity and legitimates those already working in and towards new paradigms. The *personalised educational landscape* would be at the *centre of social policy* and justifiably subject to necessary funding. Many of the current agendas – *Every Child Matters, Building Schools for the Future,* and *Extended Schools* along with *Personalisation* can all be re-orientated to support the paradigm shift advocated here.

The *model of change is based on continuous adaptation, is organic, network-based and viral.* It creates its own dynamic because people will recognise the advantages and possibilities because empowered, motivated people will stay engaged and make it work.

The prize of personalisation is incalculable. *Taking choice seriously* allows us to support the reshaping of our society in ways that reflect basic human, needs, rights and responsibilities. It offers an adaptive and unifying vision focusing at the heart of what it is to be educated, and to share in the qualitative aspects of life and work. Its success will be evidenced in lives, work and learning careers; in the biographies, health and contribution of individuals; in the strength of families and communities and the rapidity of how we address sustainability, poverty, disengagement, crime, personal and social disintegration.

References and selected bibliography

Abbott, J. (1999) *The Child is Father of the Man*, Bath: The 21st Century Learning Initiative.

Abbott, J. and Ryan, T. (2000) *The Unfinished Revolution*, Stafford: The Network Educational Press.

Adcock, J. (1995) *In Place of Schools*, London: New Education Press.

Adock, J. (2000) *Teaching Tomorrow, personal tuition as an alternative to school*, Nottingham: Education Now Books.

Arthur Andersen and Creative Learning Systems (1999) *School of the Future Presentations*, Arthur Andersen and *Creative Learning Systems*.

Attwell, G. (2007) *The Personalised Learning Environment: The future of eLearning?* ELearning Papers, Vol 2 no.1. ISSN:1887-1542 www.elearningpapers.eu accessed December 2007.

Barson, L. (2006) *Learner-Managed Learning and Home-based Education: A European Perspective*, Nottingham: Educational Heretics Press and Learning Unlimited.

Bentley, T. and Miller, R. (2006) *Getting the Questions Right,* in OECD / CERI (2006).

Bentley, T. and Wilsdon, J. (2003) *The Adaptive State: strategies for personalising the public realm*, London: Demos.

Bernstein, E. (2007) *The Secret Revolution: A psychologist's adventures in education*, Victoria: Canada & Oxford, Trafford Publishing.

Cameron, B. (1995) *Extension to the Declaration of Learner Rights and Responsibilities*, http://www.wondertree.org accessed December 2007.

Cunningham, I. *Self-Managed Learning: Publications and Papers* http://www.selfmanagedlearning.org/publicat.htm accessed December 2007.

Fortune-Wood, J. (2000) *Doing it their way: Home-based education and autonomous learning,* Nottingham: Educational Heretics Press.

Fortune-Wood, J. (2001) *Bound to be Free: Home education as a positive alternative to paying the hidden costs of 'free' education,* Nottingham: Educational Heretics Press.

Fortune-Wood, M. (2005) *The Face of Home-based Education 1: Who, why and how,* Nottingham: Educational Heretics Press.

Gilbert, C. et al. (2006) *2020 Vision Report of the Teaching and Learning in 2020 Review Group,* http://www.teachernet.gov.uk/docbank/index.cfm?id=107 accessed December 2007.

Goodman, P. (1962) *Compulsory Miseducation,* Harmondsworth: Penguin.

Glines, D. (2002) *Educational Alternatives for Everyone: A handbook for educators, families politicians,* St Paul, Minnesota: The International Association for Learning Alternatives (IALA).

Glines, D. (2006) *Personalising Education and Year Round Learning: Yesterday, today and tomorrow,* in The Journal of Personalised Education Now Issue 4. CPE/PEN

Green, H., Facer, K., Rudd, T., Dillon, P. and Humphreys, P. (2005) *Personalisation and Digital Technologies,* Bristol: Futurelab www.futurelab.org.uk/research/personalisation.htm.

Holt, J. (1982) *Teach Your Own,* Brightlingsea: Lighthouse Books.

Humphreys, P (2004) *Personalised Education,* in Personalised Education:The Journal of Personalised Education Now. Issue 1. Nottingham. Centre for Personalised Education Trust.

Humphreys, P (2004a) *Imagine a Learning City,* Unpublished manuscript

Humphreys, P (2004b) *Principles of Personalisation,* on Personalised Education Now website http://c.person.ed.gn.apc.org /

Humphreys, P (2005) *Personalised Education: A Framework for Evaluation,* Unpublished manuscript

Humphreys, P edit (2007) 'Recycling Schools' - Special Issue 6, *Personalised Education-The Journal of Personalised Education Now,* Nottingham: Centre for Personalised Education Trust.

Humphreys, P (2007) '8 Principles of Personalisation', in *Personalised Education: The Journal of Personalised Education Now,* Recycling Schools Special Issue 6, Nottingham: Centre for Personalised Education Trust.

Humphreys, P. (forthcoming) *The Freethinker's Guide to Personalisation* (working title), Nottingham:Educational Heretics Press.

Illich, I. (1971) *Deschooling Society,* Harmondsworth: Penguin.

Jeffs, T. and Smith, M.K. (2005) *Informal Education: Conversation, democracy and learning,* Nottingham: Educational Heretics Press.

Kellet, M. (2005) *Children as Active Researchers: a new research paradigm for the 21st century?* ERSC: http://www.ncrm.ac.uk/publications/methodsrevie w/MethodsReviewPaperNCRM-003.pdf accessed December 2007

Leadbeater, C. (2004) *Learning About Personalisation,* London: Demos.

Leadbeater, C. (2005) *Personalisation Through Participation: A new script for public services,* London: Demos.

Meighan, R. (1988) Flexi-schooling: Education for tomorrow, starting yesterday, Ticknall: Education Now Books.

Meighan, R. (1997) *The Next Learning System,* Nottingham: Educational Heretics Press.

Meighan, R. (2001) (Edit) *25 years of home-based education: Research, Reviews and Case Material,* Nottingham: Education Now Books.

Meighan, R. (2005) *Comparing Learning System: the good, the bad, the ugly and the counter-productive,* Nottingham: Educational Heretics Press.

Meighan, R. (ed.) (2004) *Damage Limitation: Trying to reduce the harm schools do to children,* Nottingham: Educational Heretics Press.

Meighan, R. and Harber, C. (2007) *A Sociology of Educating,* London: Continuum.

Miller, R. (ed.) (2000) *Creating Learning Communities: Models, resources and new ways of thinking about teaching and learning,* Foundation for Educational Renewal, Brandon, Vermont USA: Solomon Press.

OECD/CERI (2006) *Personalising Education,* OECD.

Puttnam, D. Lord (2007) 'In class I have to power down', *Education Guardian* 8th May 2007.

Priesnitz, W. (2000) 'Education Can Lead the Way to a Sustainable Society' in Miller, R. (ed.).

Reimer, E. (1971) *The School is Dead,* Harmondsworth: Penguin.

Rudd, T., Colligan, F. and Naik, R. (2006) *Learner Voice: A handbook from Futurelab,* Bristol: Futurelab.

Rudd, T. Gifford, C. Morrison, J. and Facer, K. (October 2006) *An Opening Education report from Futurelab,*
http://www.futurelab.org.uk/research/openingeducation.htm
PDF report:
http://www.futurelab.org.uk/download/pdfs/research/opening_education/Learning_Spaces_report.pdf
Web version:
http://www.futurelab.org.uk/research/openingeducation/learning_spaces_01.htm
accessed December 2007

Rudd, T., Sutch, D. and Facer, K. (2006) *Towards New Learning Networks - an pening Education report from Futurelab,* Bristol. Futurelab.

Shute, C. (1993) *Compulsory Schooling Disease - how children absorb fascist values,* Nottingham: Educational Heretics Press.

Webb, J. (1999) *Those Unschooled Minds - how home-educated children grow up,* Nottingham: Educational Heretics Press.

Webster, M. and Buglass, G. (2005) *Finding Voices, Making Choices,* Nottingham: Educational Heretics Press.

Williamson, B. (2005) *Young people as researchers,* Futurelab Viewpoint Article http://www.futurelab.org.uk/viewpoint/art52.htm accessed December 2007.

Wikipedia Web 2.0: http://en.wikipedia.org/wiki/Web_2 accessed December 2007

Wondertree Foundation (1995) *Declaration of Learner Rights and Responsibilities,* http://www.wondertree.org accessed December 2007

CO-OPERATIVE LEARNING DEBRIEFING STAGES – diagram 1

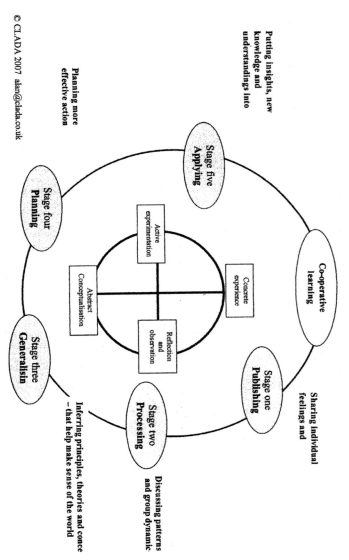

Co-operative learning

Sharing individual feelings and

Putting insights, new knowledge and understandings into

Stage five Applying

Stage four Planning

Planning more effective action

Active experimentation

Concrete experience

Abstract Conceptualisation

Reflection and observation

Stage three Generalisin

Stage two Processing

Stage one Publishing

Discussing patterns and group dynamic

Inferring principles, theories and conce – that help make sense of the world

Chapter three

Learning co-operatively

by Alan Wilkins

"Learning to co-operate, co-operating to learn"
(Slavin 1985)

Extract

We live in a complex society, comprising diverse cultures, varied belief systems and ethnic backgrounds. This cosmopolitan montage creates a wonderful array of connections, experiences and sensations of being with others and living interesting and meaningful lives. Woven into this matrix are social, economic and political strands that add to the complexity of being a citizen and making sense of our own identity, place and role. It is no longer appropriate to juxtapose notions of competitiveness (often perceived as a strength; I win, you lose) with co-operation (often perceived as a weakness; I win, you win, we win). The competitive ideological precept becomes tenuous with a close analysis of our dynamic multifarious culture. There are a myriad of interlocking groups that necessarily need to interact with one another in order for our society to function - families, peer and friendship networks, 'face book' (for the new social networking internet generation), whole communities and complex institutions and systems. This requires sophisticated sets of social skills built upon a foundation of self-confidence and self esteem. The premise of this chapter is that being able to develop co-operative understanding and skills is an entitlement for all young people and for older persons too. There is an opportunity to bring co-operative learning ideals and techniques to the educational foreground, yet to do so requires a fuller understanding of the values that underpin co-operation, and how such a value systems guides co-operative educational theory and practice.

Context

The co-operative ethic is not new in the United Kingdom; it precedes the 19th century establishment of the large industrial and co-operative societies that emerged across the UK from 1844 onwards reaching a peak in the 1950s. Hundreds of mutual social formations emerged and failed during the 18th century as people experimented with friendly societies, burial clubs, mill societies and stores; it is possible to look back further and identify mutual aid in earlier more primitive societies, in medieval cities and in pastoral communities that lived and worked collectively to ensure the fundamentals for survival (Kropotkin 1902)

Co-operation – latent and manifest social behaviour

Co-operation is implicitly a collective act. In modern society is possible to identify at least five forms of co-operation:

- *Automatic co-operation* exists where strangers coalesce around a particular threat, action, place, or procedure (such as funnelling through a confined space or moving onto an escalator), they automatically, without conscious thought, move physically in accordance with one another to enable all to move through the restricted opening. It is unplanned, involves little or no communication and is not noticed

- *Spontaneous co-operation* is those actions taken by neighbours and friends; they do not consciously think about the fact that they are helping someone else - they spontaneously do it (they give lifts, fix cars, they share materials, resources and food). It is unstated and voluntary.

- *Traditional co-operation* describes more established communal action based on social norms; particularly agricultural (18th century villagers needed to work collectively to survive; bringing in the harvest, planting food, looking after cattle). All contributed to the community's survival and latent forms are evident in rural settings; though it is evident in urban environments too. Most major religions and older world cultures express this form based on moral obligation; rejecting or refusing to conform often leads to ostracism and expulsion.

- *Directed co-operation* is an emergent form; that initially appears contradictory. Individuals become focused on a particular goal; membership is initially voluntary but then collective survival demands conformity to a set of rules or regulations that are guidelines that partially or completely inhibit individual action (being in a sport's team or a soldier in an army platoon engaged in a military exercise). Large hierarchical organisations implicitly adhere to and expect this form of co-operation. The financial institutions need to agree to principles of action; they co-operate within a competitive setting; everyone within that group requires the support and assistance of others. There is interdependence, otherwise the whole system fails.

- *Contractual co-operation* is more evident. There is a voluntaristic and formal dimension that includes local associations, such a tenants and allotment clubs, mutual assistance through babysitting circles and buying groups. Much larger legal entities are the co-operative retail societies, credit unions and worker co-operatives (in the UK and internationally). All forms enable members to contractually work together for a common goal or need. (Nisbet 1968, Craig 1993)

Co-operation is everywhere; it is a concrete experience, not just a theoretical concept. Co-operation is in the very essence of our being. There is evidence in contemporary society that co-operation is part of almost every aspect of our lives.

The current educational context

The last two decades of education in United Kingdom, with a preoccupation on the national curriculum core elements of education and knowledge, target driven grading and school league tables, has restricted the time for enrichment, extracurricular sports and social activities. This has consequentially reduced the opportunities for young people to collectively work and learn together.

More recently new preoccupations have emerged with vocational learning to enhance the UK skill base in order to build the capacity of the state to maintain economic advantage in the global economic market. There is now an emphasis on personal, learning and thinking skills, enterprise and the advent of citizenship pre 16 and post 16 of which the youth voice is just one element (QCA 2004), (Crick 1998 and 2000). Other developments include personal social health education, the drive to encourage youth volunteering, reformulations of established youth organisations (Duke of Edinburgh's Award, Scouts and Guides) and the more recent government policy enactments and committee reports (*Every Child Matters,* the Ajegbo *'Diversity and Identity'* report, and *'Our Shared Future'*). These, together with the introduction of the new secondary curriculum in 2008 (QCA 2008), collectively create a new opportunity for more co-operative and collective forms of learning. This should enable young people to be consulted, have status, make choices and to have their voices heard.

However, the majority of the current body of teachers have not experienced teacher training programmes that explore co-operative facilitation styles or methods. There is a lot of catching up to do to build the competences needed to design innovative learning programmes that engage learners as a group as well as individuals. Programmes that create a learning dynamic in which new interpretations are generated by more people working on agreed topics and in agreed ways, result in a collective sharing of outcomes for everyone's benefit.

Identity, citizenship and community cohesion

British society is on the move. In 2006 400,00 people left permanently to live and work abroad; 591,000 arrived to work and learn. The Commission for Integration and Cohesion notes that community tension is not only related to ethnicity and faith, but with different cultures, intergeneration, gender and social class issues.

In 2005 Trevor Phillips, the then Chair of the Commission for Racial Equality, warned that Britain was *"sleepwalking its way into segregation"* (Phillips 2005). Since then the emphasis has been shifting from the differences that divide people to what brings people together and the need for community cohesion for a stable and safe society of the future. *"Cohesion is principally the process that must happen in all communities to ensure different groups of people get on well together; whilst integration is principally the process that ensures new residents and existing residents adapt to one another"*. (CIC 2007)

A fundamental idea associated with this is identity, as Sir Keith Ajegbo states, *"none of us exists in one dimension. ... We live in sophisticated times and we have repertoires to inhabit many different worlds and multiple identitie'"* (QIA 2008). Young people constantly strive to make sense of themselves and the society in which they live. This is an ongoing challenge for all people throughout their lives, as is the process of interaction; being in social company and surviving there.

In this context co-operative learning has a significant role to play in our contemporary future. It can assist the building of multiple cohesive communities, emphasising what we have and can do in common, rather than what makes us different. Co-operative learning also contributes to the evolving citizenship education processes now regarded as an important foundation to the new secondary curriculum being launched in September 2008.

The co-operative learning opportunity

Co-operative learning is not a new idea or method. Extensive exploration of the co-operative learning approach is evident in the United States (Johnson and Johnson 1993, Kagen 1994), Israel (Hertz-Lazarowitz 1992), the United Kingdom (Wilkins 1988) and other European states such as Sweden and Finland. The unique co-operative learning perspective emergent in the United Kingdom is the direct association with the co-operative movement. Significant strides were made in the 1980s alongside the exploratory schools-industry curriculum project that resulted in the economic and industrial understanding cross-curricular theme (Smith 1988). A vibrant network of co-operative educators continues to expand today. The establishment of co-operative school trusts (Wilson and Mills 2007), school based INSET and whole cohort events (promoting positive behaviours, fair-trade, school-based co-operative businesses, forming social enterprises) all contribute to the potential to link learning activities within schools, youth groups and home-based learning to the ideals and practices of the co-operative movement.

Co-operative values make the difference

Behind the co-operative movement (within the United Kingdom and throughout the world) is a basic tenant of values. The ten values are distinct yet connected to each other; it is this combination and each values definition that make them unique to co-operatives and to co-operators.

The six organisational values:

- Self-help
- Self responsibility
- Democracy

- Equality
- Equity
- Solidarity

The four ethical values:

- Honesty
- Openness
- Social Responsibility
- Caring for others

These values are the fundamental beliefs that underpin co-operative learning and must be understood before exploring the relationship with and between facilitation, behaviour and structures. Plenary sessions at recent co-operative learning conferences held in England explored the fit between co-operative and educational values and discovered a close alignment.

The first six values define co-operatives as a special form of organisation. 'Self-help' is the belief that all people in society have the ability to develop themselves as individuals and in harmony with others to work and live together to mutual benefit. Forming, running or joining a co-operative is the ultimate expression. This form of co-ownership closely associates with ideas about multiple intelligence (Gardner 1993) and learning style theory (Kolb 1972). It is the belief that people are different and have different capacities that can be developed. People have different learning styles and different intelligences, none better or worse, they are merely different. In our modern world we need all these capabilities developed to their full potential with a heightened awareness of the ability of others and the capacity to work with them.

Aligned with 'self-help is 'self-responsibility' – each taking responsibility to contribute and to develop their skills, knowledge and understanding (through education, training and application) to contribute to the successful functioning and creation of the co-operative organisation or business. 'Self-responsibility' alludes to the co-operative fact that that it is the co-operative, and all associated with it, not the government or a wealthy benefactor, that meets the collective need - we cannot rely on others to do what we should do for ourselves. We each have a responsibility to make a contribution whether it is to the family, friendship network, school or workplace.

At the heart of any co-operative is the core value of 'Democracy'. Co-operators endeavour to act democratically, through consultation, collective agreement and through representation to ensure that all have their say to influence a co-operative's policy and activity. All individuals within a diverse community have a right to express their ideas and be listened to. It is through open debate and dialogue that the right conclusions are reached to the betterment of all.

The genuine enactment of 'Equality' ensures that anyone, member or worker, can participate and contribute to their meritocratic best from a position of equal status.

'Equity' emphasises justice and the preservation of fairness in access to resources and training, and reward for contribution and patronage.

The premise of 'Solidarity' is that working together for collective and mutual benefit is ultimately more productive than working alone.

There are four ethical values associated with the co-operative movement that may be found in other organisations but are fundamental to the practice of being a co-operator. 'Honesty' relates to the endeavour to be truthful, an absolute. 'Openness' is the intention to inform and disclose so all participating or affected by a collective endeavour are able to participate and understand why and what is taking place. The last two ethical values are interdependent - 'Social responsibility' originates from the close association that co-operatives have always had with the communities from which they emerged, whilst 'Caring for others' recognises the importance of relationships between people, not items or numbers, rather a genuine care towards another human person as a member of humanity who ever they are.

Any educator making a comparative analysis of the co-operative value system and that of education will note the many correlations between their endeavour as an educator and to those associated with the co-operative movement. All 10 values are significant and together they define the difference between a co-operative and any other organisation.

Co-operative learning as experiential learning

Co-operative learning is both active and collective, and is by implication experiential. The experiential learning cycle starts with 1) a concrete experience, this is 2) reflected upon to understand the experience both as an individual and as a collective dynamic (this engages in feelings and personal enlightenment) and then 3) a theoretical and conceptual process generically makes sense of the experience holistically, which is then translated into 4) a series of recommendations or insights that guide future action, activity or behaviour (Pfeiffer and Jones 1980).

(See Diagram overleaf)

Diagram 1
Co-operative learning debriefing stages

PERSONALISED EDUCATION: A FRAMEWORK FOR EVALUATION

5 Point Scale - Degree Of Personalisation - Scale refers to 'wholly' or 'mainly'. Responses should be best fit.

Fig.1 (Humphreys, 2005)

EIGHT PERSONALISED EDUCATION PRINCIPLES / > % Approximation >	None 0%	Emergent (shallow) 1% - 25%	Developing (shallow) 26% - 50%	Developed (shallow/deep) 51% - 75%	Established (deep) 76% - 100%
1. Degree of LEARNER CONTROL: Personalisation needs learner-managed and co-constructed learning	Learning imposed and controlled	^	^	^	Learner – led and co-constructed
2. Degree of LEARNER DEPENDENCY: Personalisation needs a shift from dependancy to independence and interdependency	Learner is totally dependent on others	^	^	^	Learner is independent and interdependent
3. Degree of LEARNER CHOICE: Personalisation needs invitational learning and assessment	Learning is imposed	^	^	^	Learning is invitational
4. Degree of EDIVERSITY: Personalisation needs learning from a personalised educational landscape of opportunities	Learning is limited to one closed setting	^	^	^	Learning from an educational landscape of opportunities
5. Degree of INTEGRATION: Personalisation needs re-integration of learning, life and community	Learning is separate and divorced from aspects of life / community	^	^	^	Learning is from other aspects of life and community
6. Degree of DEMOCRACY: Personalisation needs democratic values, organization and practice	Authoritarian values, organization and practice	^	^	^	Democratic values, organization and practice
7. Degree of CURRICULUM CONTROL: Personalisation needs catalogue and natural versions of curriculum and assessment	Imposed Curricula	^	^	^	Catalogue and natural versions of curriculum and assessment
8. Degree of AGE LINKAGE: Personalisation needs the de-coupling of age-stage progressions and assessments	Age – stage progression and assessment	^	^	^	Life-long learning related to readiness to learn

Co-operative group developmental processes

Co-operation is human activity that can be recognised as living, working or learning in groups. There has been much research into team working and group working (Tuckman 1970, Sanford 1980). Groups do not just exist, they evolve and develop; some are unfacilitated, others facilitated. Co-operative groups are usually internally facilitated and travel through a developmental process. Sanford re-orders Tuckman's model (that relates to unfacilitated groups) into a five-stage process (Forming, *norming, storming*, performing and adjourning). When co-operative learning groups first come together they are either self-facilitated or have an external learning mediator/facilitator; they establish norms (agreements on why they exist, how they will function and what they seek to achieve). This leads onto a new familiarity between group members and a less guarded expression of views and differences that brings the group into a healthy stage of conflict; the storming. A group that manages to resolve internal issues through revisiting and revising the norms through open and direct exchange of views will emerge as a high performance group. Most groups, particularly in educational settings, will at some stage come to a termination and this moment should be recognised and celebrated.

Another distinction of a co-operative learning group is the negotiation of what is learned; this can involve two persons (the learner and a learning mediator), or a whole group (self directed or in partnership with the learning mediator). Whatever the format, the group will still go through a process of change. The group dynamic will necessarily comprise three parallel levels of activity from setting out on the task till its completion – 1) an *action schedule* of agreed functional matters that include time, functional roles of co-ordinator, scribe, etc; 2) the actual completion of *the task, the activity;* and 3) the underlying *process of interaction.* (Cockman et al 1998). It is this *process* dimension that is often over looked and is particularly relevant to co-operative groups - processing the realm of active listening, building on contributions, sensitivity to the feelings of others, suspending judgement, living with ambiguity, open decision making. As the group becomes more adept and its members gain confidence, the group becomes more able to lead itself.

Given this understanding the learning mediator/facilitator role will change from an external directive function to ultimately a participant learner. Being able to adapt to this changing group dynamic is the art of being an educator and facilitator of learning.

These considerations must influence the design of the learning programme itself. Whilst the negotiation of the purpose and outcomes of the learning is a given; how the learning takes place is not necessarily the preserve of the learner; the ways to interact with the resources, share insights and build the collective understanding must be a responsibility of the learning mediator until the group is adept in arranging their learning and information sharing processes for itself.

This is the realm of active learning techniques. The use of different structures to frame the learning activity, such as paper and discussion carousels, jigsaw grouping methods, value continuums, energisers and review methods (see Kagan 2002, Dynamix 2003, Ginnis 2002). All these techniques are informed by learning and intelligence theories and recent research into how the brain works. Active co-operative learning is the preserve of co-operative training and development organisations such as CLADA, Dynamix and First Question (see details below), all experimenting with the application of existing ideas and techniques whilst devising and creating new activities and methods.

The interconnections between values, behaviour and structure

Young people working co-operatively are not just a collection of individuals sitting in the same space, they are interacting and they are interdependent, working with as well as alongside one another. This requires sophisticated human and social interaction skills, emotional intelligence, and a value consciousness. We know that learners learn best when they are confident and have high self-esteem. We know that learning environments should be visual, auditory and kinaesthetic (Smith 1996). We know that there is a cycle of learning in which experience is built upon through reflection, theoretical generalisations and an application of that insight to new experiences and new challenges (Kolb 1972, Fenwick 2003).

There must be a harmonious balance between the values that guide the behaviour which in turn needs an appropriate structure to enable the values and behaviour to be fully expressed.

Personalised co-operative learning – links with citizenship and enterprise

The current focus on citizenship education and active citizenship are critical steps towards assisting young people to shape and make sense of their world. As populations increase, space becomes more congested and there is heightened competition for scarce resources. Migration, unification (in Europe and beyond) and globalisation demand that all within a society are capable of developing more complex understandings of the concept of 'community'.

Those pursuing democratic education have stressed the importance of hearing the youth voice. Today young people have more opportunity to express their view as customers of learning and services through college/school councils, youth forums and consultations. This requires the development of new skills and new capacities to critically review and constructively find solutions, make informed suggestions and recommendations for the future. Recent developments, including citizenship in pre 16 school programmes (Crick 2001) and a concerted emphasis on active citizenship promoted by the Post 16 Citizenship Support Programme (LSN 2007) have paved a way to enable educators and learners to engage with democratic practice. This may still be a shallow expression of democratic practice (Meighan 2001) but it enables all to experiment and engage with the concept and enactment of democracy.

Creating space and opportunity for young people to form social and co-operative enterprises seems an obvious extension to the ideas expressed above whilst contributing to the current enterprise education agenda.

A commercial and industrial literacy perspective would accept that a competency to co-operate is fundamental to a civilised society, and that the educational and learning system must incorporate opportunities for young people to learn to work co-operatively together. Young people are entitled to access information about all economic, industrial and organisational forms and values, to empower them to formulate their own informed opinion and understanding. Co-operative enterprise activities offer another way to provide this opportunity.

Students can engage with and learn more about democracy, the issues of equality, mutual interest and mutual participation as well as understanding the importance of making surpluses for the sustainability of a business or community benefit. Achieving the task is not the sole measure of success.

Co-operative enterprises are real businesses, but they are different from the standard conventional limited company model. In all businesses economic, industrial and commercial understanding is a prerequisite for those in management, productive and administrative roles. They need to work collaboratively in order to make the enterprise a success. Co-operatives are no different in this respect but are formulated and structured differently. It is interesting that when young people are given a choice of business structure they nearly always choose a co-operative model (an endorsement of the automatic/spontaneous forms of co-operation described earlier).

Choosing to learn and work co-operatively – in conclusion

Whatever the past or present emphasis within British society on competition or individualism, our multiple cultures encourage and recognise co-operative behaviour as important for social development. In our society the ability to co-operate is crucial. Social interaction within the group is a microcosm of inter-group and inter-societal relationships. The process by which individuals work together as a group to solve a problem or a task in a co-operative learning community is equally important. Participating in this way young people experience co-operation as a process, gaining an understanding of co-operative values in action. Co-operative models provide the context to bring life and an added dimension to enterprise learning. They give young people opportunities to further develop the knowledge, understanding and skills necessary to be an active contributor to, participant in and shaper of society with the added dimension of mutual benefit and social goals. Being able to constructively and creatively handle problems in social settings is a necessary life skill at the core of living and working together in the twenty-first century. Learning co-operatively is a serious and effective choice.

References

Craig J (1993) *The Nature of Co-operation*, Quebec: Black Rose Books

Crick B (1998) *Education for citizenship and the teaching of democracy in schools* – final report of the advisory group on citizenship: QCA

Crick B (2000) *Citizenship for 16-19 year olds in education and training* – report of advisory group to secretary of state for education and employment: FEFC

Cockman P, Evans B and Reynolds P (1999) *Consultation for real people: a client centred approach for change agents and leaders,* pg 53 Berkshire: McGraw-Hill

Commission on Integration and Cohesion (2007) *Our Shared Future* - CIC

Dynamix (2002) *Spice it up,* Cardiff: Save the Children Fund

Fenwick J (2003) *Learning through experience: troubling orthodoxies and intersecting questions,* Florida: Krieger publishing

Gardner H ((1984) *Frames of mind,* London: Fontana Press

Ginnis P (2002) *The teachers toolkit,* Carmarthen: Crown House Publishing

Hertz-Lazarowitz R and Miller. N (eds) (1992) *Interaction in co-operative groups: the theoretical anatomy of group learning,-* Cambridge University Press

Johnson D, Johnson R and Holubec (1993) *Circles of learning – co-operation in classrooms,* – 4th edition Minnesota: the Interaction Book Company

Kagan S (1994) *Co-operative learning,* – San Juan Capistanano: Resources for Teachers

Kolb D, Rubin I and McIntyre J (1971) *Organisational Psychology an experiential approach,* New Jersey: Prentice-Hall

Kropotkin P (1902 reprinted 1993) *Mutual Aid a factor of evolution,* London: Freedom Press

Macpherson I (1995) *The co-operative identity in the 21st century Switzerland,* International Co-operative Alliance

LSN (2007) www.post16citizenship.org

Meighan R (2005) *Comparing learning systems: the good, the bad, the ugly and the counter-productive,* Nottingham: Educational Heretics Press

Meighan R (2001) chapter on *Democratic Education,* – International Encyclopaedia of Democratic Thought

Nesbitt R (1968) *Co-operation,* International Encyclopedia of the Social Sciences vol 1 p384

Pfieffer J and Jones J eds (1980) *Introduction to structured experiences* – The 1980 annual handbook for group facilitators, California: University Associates

Phillips T (2005) http://news.bbc.co.uk/1/hi/uk/4270010.stm

QCA (2004) *Play your part – post 16 citizenship guidance* - QCA

QCA (2008) www.curriculum.qca.org.uk

QIA (2008) *Moving forward together: citizenship learning for community cohesion*, London: QIA

Slavin R et al (1985) *Learning to co-operate, co-operating to learn* – New York: Plenum Press

Smith A (1996) *Accelerated learning in the classroom*, Stafford: network educational press

Smith A (2002) *The brains behind it*, Stafford Network Educational Press

Wilkins A (1988) 'Co-operation, co-operatives and education' in Smith D (ed) *Partners in change: education-industry collaboration* – York: Longmans

Wilson M and Mills C (2007) *Co-operative values are a difference – in the curriculum and governance of schools*, - Mutuo

www.clada.co.uk

www.dynamix.ltd.uk

Chapter four

Personalised Learning and Democratic Learning Co-operatives

by Roland Meighan

Personalised learning has at least two forms. In the solo version, a learner manages their own learning and learning plan. In the group version, learners manage their learning and learning plan as a co-operative. Either approach requires that choice is taken seriously and that any tutor, if one is involved, operates as a 'guide on the side' and not the dominant 'sage on the stage'.

Democratic methods can often be seen in single families educating at home where they agree to work together on a particular project. It is also found where pairs of families or groups of families decide to work together.

Groups may also make use of the solo version of personalised learning when a group member agrees to research a theme on behalf of the group and report back, or to prepare to lead a session of the group.

Thus, in **democratic education**, the learners as a group have the power to make some, most, or even all of the key decisions, since power is shared and not appropriated in advance by a minority of one or more. Its slogan is usually summed up in the words:

"We did it our way."

In many so-called 'democratic' countries, such educational practices are rare and often meet with sustained, hostile and irrational opposition. There was the case of a UK HMI, who having witnessed a very impressive learning co-operative session, declared that he could not report it as a learning co-operative because such an idea was not on the educational map approved of by the government. *"It is off our radar,"* he explained.

The features of democratic learning can be described in the following fashion:

Discipline
is democratic discipline by working co-operatively to agreed rules and principles, rather than those imposed by the coercive principle of 'you will do it our way'.

Knowledge
is essentially the skills and information needed by the group to maintain and develop its learning programme.

Learning
is activity agreed by the group to gain experience, information or particular skills working either together or reporting-back tasks which had been delegated to individuals.

Teaching
is any activity, including formal instruction, that the group judges will lead to effective learning.

Resources
are anything appropriate to the group's research and learning including people, places, and experiences.

Location
is anywhere that the learning group can meet to pursue effective learning.

Organisation
is commonly in self-regulated groups where dialogue and co-operative learning can take place.

Assessment
is by any form of assessment, using any tests, devised by the learners or by others, that are seen to be appropriate to the situation.

Aims
are, essentially, to produce people with the confidence and skills to manage their own learning within a democratic culture.

Power
is shared in the group which is seen as responsible both individually and collectively for its exercise.

Leadership
is shared and revolves, rather than resides in one assertive person. It is expressed in the words of the ancient Chinese sage, Lao-tse:

"Of a good leader, they say, when his work is done, we did this ourselves!"

Some of the consequences of democratic learning co-operatives that have been found in the research are:

(a) that there is likely to develop a sense of community amongst a group of learners;

(b) that there develops a working partnership between appointed teachers and learners;

(c) that appointed teachers develop trust in the capability and creative ability of their fellow humans who come to them in the role of students;

(d) that dialogue becomes an essential activity rather than an optional feature, and unmandated or imposed learning is not seen as legitimate;

(e) that standards of formal work rise, with bonus skills such as increased personal confidence, higher self-esteem, and enhanced discussion and research skills.

Case Study: A Democratic Learning Co-operative in Teacher Education

Teacher education has been part of a cycle whereby authoritarian classrooms pass students on to authoritarian teacher courses, which produce authoritarian teachers who go back into schools, to sustain and perpetuate authoritarian classrooms, round and round in a closed circle. Breaking out of this cycle is not easy, even when it is seen as desirable. But if it is not broken at the learner-teacher point, teachers go into their careers with no vision of alternatives and no experience of democratic learning. It is usually more difficult to change later.

So, what happened when we tried a democratic approach on a teacher education course? After a short settling-in period, when the students had introduced each other to the group, the news was broken by the tutors, Clive Harber and Roland Meighan, that although there was a planned course ready in the familiar authoritarian expert style, there were other options open to the group. They could consider operating as a democratic learning co-operative which would devise and plan its own programme of studies using the tutors as resources if and when deemed appropriate. A specimen contract was available for discussion purposes if this option required any elaboration.

Specimen group learning contract

- We agree to accept responsibility for our course as a group.
- We agree to take an active part in the learning of the group.
- We agree to be critical, constructively, of our own and other people's ideas.
- We agree to plan our own programme of studies, implement it using the group members

and appointed teachers as resources, and review the outcomes in order that we may learn from any limitations we identify.
- We agree to the keeping of a group log-book of work completed, planning decisions, session papers and any other appropriate documents.
- We agree to share the duties of being in the chair, being meeting secretary, session organisers and contributors.
- We agree to review this contract from time to time.

The course thus began as a consultation about the approach to be adopted for the course itself. There was, in fact, another option made available to the group and that was of a mixture of approaches, e.g. adopting one approach for one term and another for another term, or some members choosing an individualised course if the majority wanted either a lecturer-taught course or a learning co-operative.

There is a need to clarify what 'a course' actually meant. In one case it referred to the 'methods of teaching' module of the Post Graduate Certificate of Education year, taking up about one third of the total time. During the period 1976 to 1991, considerable experience of this approach was accumulated as fifteen courses approached their learning in the democratic mode. One course decided to begin with the authoritarian mode and change to the democratic when they felt appropriate. This took about four weeks. This particular course was evaluated by an independent observer and an account published (Fielding et al., 1979).

In two cases, part of the course was run democratically, in one case one day a week, in another for the summer term. The majority of members of these two groups expressed regret in the end of course evaluations that they had not chosen to do the whole of their course as a learning co-operative. The tutors had to adjust to a different theory of teaching and so did most of the students. All were agreed, however, that the effort was well worthwhile. The new habits were a great improvement on the old ones.

Rationale for a democratic approach

If teaching in secondary schools in the UK is seen primarily as a decision-making activity, one appropriate way of learning to teach may be simulating the process on the training course itself by selecting the aims, content, methods and evaluation methods for their own group. In effect, teachers in training can experiment on themselves, practising many of the skills they will need for the rest of their careers, in contrast to the authoritarian approach of listening to someone else tell them how to make appropriate decisions. Since currently a central activity in secondary schools is formal instruction, students will practise this activity by taking the role of instructor to their fellow students.

In most teacher training there is a marked contrast between the essentially passive role assigned to students at the training institution and the active role on teaching practice. The adoption of a democratic approach weakens this dichotomy since the students become active in both situations.

The outcomes from the learners' viewpoint

No student involved in the fifteen courses wrote an evaluation regretting the debate over the methods they should adopt for the learning, and none of those who opted for a democratic mode has evaluated the experience negatively.

The written evaluations produced by the various group members contained a number of regular themes. One was that of confidence:

> "Democratic responsibility, as opposed to sitting back and always receiving, meant that students had to use the skills they already had, as well as learning new ones. Such a situation was a good one in which to develop confidence in one's own thinking."

Most students had something to say about motivation and always in favourable terms:

> "I felt great responsibility for the course and this involvement meant always taking a mentally active part. I felt no resentment against somebody trying to impose work or a situation on me. Thus motivation was high."

> "Personally for me the course was very stimulating theoretically and practically. I not only learnt a lot but experienced much. I felt motivated to work and get involved because I felt it was our course."

> "There was intellectual enjoyment. Intellectual exploration became an exciting and satisfying end in its own right, rather than a means to a boring and worthless end (e.g. exams, assessment, achieving the teacher's aims, etc.). Ultimately the only end was personal satisfaction, thus the only pressure was personal. Personal pressure stimulated, and made exciting, my learning. Outside pressure always deadened and stifled it."

Several students noted that the discussion techniques of the group members were utilised to the full and developed in the process:

> "The discussions were conducted on a relaxed and friendly basis and were therefore enjoyed by

most students. Most students felt able to contribute their ideas and opinions to some or all of the topics discussed. Personally I have found this aspect of the course very beneficial because it has facilitated the exchange of ideas and information between group members and the exploration of many different aspects of key issues."

One of the conventional objections to democratic learning is that the content may be deficient if the 'experts' let go of the selection of the 'best' content for the task in hand. The students did not support this interpretation:

"With all students choosing the range of subjects the content, inevitably (in my mind) was of a greater range and more relevance than if the 'teacher' had done all the choosing. A group of students, especially from different specialist backgrounds, were able to provide more resources than one teacher could."

"The standard of papers given was generally very high - probably much higher than if the work had been set by the tutor."

The democratic nature of the course meant that decision making was practised and that responsibility was shared. The students found this a favourable feature of the course:

"Responsibility and authority were dispersed among all members of the group, meaning that the assumption of these was voluntary, rather than them being concentrated into one person's (teacher) job. The taking of responsibility on a voluntary basis did not present any problems as all members of the group were happy to take it."

"A system whereby 'rules' were made, but made by ourselves as we went along, meant that the

group had security and direction, but also adaptability and flexibility."

"One was encouraged to recognise the value of other students as a resource."

"The content of the course would be decided by the group. Essentially this meant that the group decided its priorities - what the particular members of the group felt would be most useful to them as future teachers. It allowed members of the group to follow up personal interests and also allowed the group to draw upon the expertise that did exist within the group."

A regular theme that occurred in the student evaluation was that of the bridging of theory and practice. Since a dichotomy is frequently reported between those two, it is interesting to see what the learners in a democratic situation had to say about this matter:

"With regard to the 'methods' course, any gaps between theory and practice were, I think, well bridged. The peculiar nature of the course, with its options (including the more radical democratic learning co-operative) offered and put into practice, meant that we did not just talk about alternative ways of teaching and learning but to a certain, albeit perhaps limited, extent, experienced and experimented with alternative methods."

There was also comment on a related tension between the problems of preparing for survival in schools as they were, whilst considering any vision as to improvements on the status quo or alternatives to the current orthodoxy:

"The course, in practice, therefore, seemed to me to cope nicely with the idealism of educational change and the practicalities and constraints involved in operationalizing such

changes. *In this way the course provided a realistic 'vision' for changed procedures in teaching while not ignoring the problems of practice, or survival, which face all teachers."*

"The experience of a democratic learning co-operative is valuable in itself for intending teachers since it presents them with an alternative method of learning and teaching for future use with their own pupils. Unless this is actually experienced by students, it is unlikely that this important innovation will reach schools in any significant degree."

"One of the roles of teacher training should be to investigate and experiment with alternative methods of teaching and learning, in a practical way, and to provide working models of the alternative methods."

The co-operative outlook to learning which is basic to the democratic approach extended in influence beyond the methods course in the university to the teaching practice situation:

"During the major Teaching Practice and in other instances the co-operative tended to be very supportive and relationships proved to be advantageous, especially during the ten long weeks of teaching practice in the spring term."

Most of the evaluations concluded with an overall verdict on the course:

"The group enjoyed the Methods Course very much. It was extremely beneficial both academically and practically. Highlights and reservations along with possible improvements and alterations were suggested, and a general report on the course was made which had the consent of the whole group."

"I hope other groups will learn from our experiences and enjoy their year as much as I believe our course has."

"The co-operative spent many hours in discussion and formulated opinions and views (often varying) in relation to our timetable of work. All the group members felt without any reservation whatsoever that the co-op was a new working experience which was stimulating, enjoyable and very worthwhile. We all gained an enormous amount from it, academically and in relation to the new relationships we formed. Everyone in the working co-operative agreed that it was an invaluable, exciting experience and one which we would advise any PGCE students to take part in regardless of discipline."

The outcomes from the tutors' point of view

The tutor involved in the first attempts and the second tutor involved later kept personal notes week by week on the democratic learning co-operatives. Some of the themes that are selected from these notes as significant are as follows.

A potential conflict was seen in the transfer from the democratic course to the authoritarian schools in which teaching practice took place. The tutors were surprised at the pay-off from the course, which seemed to more than offset any expected responses of alienation and rejection. The students approached the Teaching Practice with considerable confidence, and this was remarked upon by the teachers in the school. Since the students were used to making decisions about what to learn and how, assembling appropriate materials and using them, they appeared to transfer these behaviours to school scheme and lesson preparation without any nervousness. They were also used to working co-operatively and so fitted into team situations with teachers with relative ease.

The tutors had to adjust to a different theory of teaching since they had been educated in authoritarian styles. They had to learn to listen much more, learn to resist the previous habit of dominating the decision-making and discussions. The facilitative role was demanding since making contacts, identifying resources and solving operational problems on the spot or at short notice were different experiences to the authoritarian approach (where, having made the decisions as to content in advance, a tutor was in a position to produce handouts and identify resources some time beforehand). The tutors also had to cope with their ideas and suggestions being either rejected or scrutinised closely and justification requested.

There were tensions with the other courses that the students were required to attend as part of their PGCE year. The confidence of members of the learning co-operative in challenging other tutors in formal lectures was not always welcome, and other students did not always find their enthusiasm and commitment appealing. On one occasion there was a joint session with another methods group to work with a visiting speaker. When she phoned to say she was unable to come due to a school crisis, the learning co-operative immediately set about organising a substitute programme for the morning for themselves. The other student teachers group declined to take part or devise something similar for themselves and went away to take the morning off with some parting remarks about the others being far too keen.

Any anxieties the tutors had about the quality of student input or the 'covering of key topics' proved groundless. The students exceeded what the tutors had planned and added ideas that had not been included, so that the tutors were learning new material in some of the sessions.

The tutors were curious as to how the students would cope with applications for posts and interviews. However, the pay-off from the course appeared to be positive rather than negative. The approach of the students seemed to appeal to many interviewers. Some head teachers have responded to the effect that 'this is a whole new generation of teachers, articulate, enthusiastic, industrious and challenging'.

Conclusion

If democratic ideologies of education have in common a view of independence in the teacher-learner relationship, the outcome is a type of power sharing and an exercise in freedom in the sense that Wright Mills (1959) expounded:

> "Freedom is, first of all, the chance to formulate the available choices, to argue over them and then the opportunity to choose. That is why freedom cannot exist without an enlarged role of human reason in human affairs."

The democratic learning co-operatives approach appears to exemplify this principle and also allow a bridging back into the authoritarian situations of schools with positive effects, so that the student teachers appeared to be well prepared to cope with schools as they are, but also having experiences and visions of possible alternatives and possible modifications to the status quo should the situation allow or require them.

Democratic learning co-operatives have also been found in the past in Primary teacher education, (Janet Meighan at the University of Derby), and in

Business Studies courses at Sunderland, in Community Arts group in Walsall (with Mark Webster and others), in home-based education learning groups, such as *The Otherwise Club* in London and the *Learning Zone* in the Isle of Wight, the *Centre for Self-Managed Learning* at Brighton under the direction of Professor Ian Cunningham, and finally in the training of doctors at the medical faculty at Chicago University.

(Case studies of DLCs in schools and in home-based education and elsewhere are given in chapter 7 of **Comparing Learning Systems** *by Roland Meighan, Educational Heretics Press, 2006)*

Chapter five

The Otherwise Club: An Invitational Learning Community

by Leslie Safran

Introduction

There is a limit to what can be learned from knowing the history of one home education invitational learning community. Each group and its situation is unique. But although in specific concrete terms there is little to learn from another group's experiences, it is possible to learn something. There are several guiding principles that are relevant to all groups and this article will make an attempt to tease them out.

Before beginning to examine these principles it will be useful to explain something about how *The Otherwise Club* began and how it works as an invitational learning centre so that the extrapolated principles are put into a context.

An Invitational Learning Community

The Otherwise Club was formed in February 1993. It is based in Brent, northwest London and supports families who choose to educate their children out of school for a variety of reasons including ideological views about education, problems at school, or special educational needs. The club was started with the purpose of aiding older children as home education is less difficult when children are aged up to about eight years old. Up to that age they enjoy being at home and engaging in family activities like visiting the park and making food. They learn an enormous amount from these every day activities. Often at about eight years old children tend to want to be with others and as they are now physically larger in size and more mentally capable, it is often difficult for families to have many over-eights in their homes. While you might be able to have one, two or even three over-eights painting on your kitchen table, having ten would be a very different matter. Further, the type of activities available at home is limited. With this is mind, the club was started in order to provide a space for lots of children to engage together in various activities, including messy play, and to participate in group activities that are not so easy to do in a home setting such as drama. In addition, it seemed that children aged between nine and thirteen, particularly girls, missed the society of others in their age group. This often translates into children wanting to go to school where they may find a larger group of friends. Although the club does not run everyday it has been able, for many children, to satisfy these needs.

The club provides a regular meeting place for families, has a small café and has collected an alternative education library. It has a lot of equipment and craft items that members can access as they wish. There is also the space for spontaneous activities as well as planned ones. It holds regular workshops such as drama, karate, drawing and history. It provides classes for those who chose to join them such as Latin for beginners and GCSEs. It promotes special events and group activities such as robot building, puppet making, felt making, visits from police dog handlers, making videos and singing and playing music together. It organises various educational outings to such places as The Tower of London, The Chiltern Open Air Museum, and so on. It runs a Duke of Edinburgh Award group for the older children with eight recently receiving their bronze award and thirteen beginning the silver award in Jan 06. The club also edits and produces a monthly newsletter for home educators across Britain and Europe called *Choice in Education*.

The title of this article describes *The Otherwise Club* as an 'invitational learning community'. This needs to be explained. Firstly, the club is not invitational in the sense that it requires one to be invited to join it although families do need to have a child of school age not at school to be able to attend. It is invitational in the sense that there is no compulsion to be a member or having become a member, to join any of the activities that the club offers. The club provides a space which invites members to use it to do any activity they wish or to do nothing at all. Doing nothing can be fruitful; it is restful, confers dignity, removes pressure and allows people to think for themselves. This 'not doing' is important because it is often difficult for people of any age, but particularly for those who have been trained throughout their life to do as they are told, to be able to be self determining. Always having activities laid out and having a schedule, even if it is a self-imposed schedule, denies the chance to experience the joy of simply living and being with friends without any defined activity. For the club, 'not doing' is as important as 'doing' and is implied by the principle of self determination.

The process of initiating a new activity at the club begins when a member places a message on a notice board suggesting an activity or class that they or someone they know can offer or would like to see offered. They include the date, time and costs. Anyone who would like to engage in that activity signs up for it. If there are enough people to cover the costs then the activity goes ahead. The criterion for signing up is interest not age. In this way the invitational nature of the club is promoted in its daily routine as well as in its over all ethos.

Secondly, it is part of the implicit educational philosophy of the club that learning takes place all the time. It is only **what** people learn that can be directed to some extent (For a more detailed analysis of what self-directed learning entails see, Safran, 2001). At *The Otherwise Club* learning is left up to the individual whatever their age. In society, many children and young people are in a situation that looks like a classroom and this is seen by most people as a place where learning takes place. But in this situation the 'learner' often learns something other than what the 'teacher' means them to learn, such as 'this is boring' or 'I am bad (or good) at some subject' or that learning only takes places at a certain time and place and with someone who is a professional doling out a monitored curriculum in small chunks. At *The Otherwise Club* this style of learning is replaced by a style that is continuous and learner driven. It would be accurate to take 'learning' out of the title 'invitational learning community' as the principle of the club is that learning takes place all the time and not just when attending an 'educational institution' or, indeed, the club. However, it is important to leave it there if only to raise this issue.

Finally, the use of the word 'community' highlights a most important part of the club's purpose both educationally and socially. The club operates through working, playing and being together:

through 'lived practice' in the community, we get to know each other including the children, we share problems and projects, we experience good and bad times, we argue and get over arguments, we see each other's children grow up, we support each other as our roles change, and we learn tolerance and patience between children, adults and children and adults. All this develops community which is the corner stone needed to put the other principles into action.

The importance of the nature of the club is increased by the marginal nature of home education and by the consequent emotional state of many people coming for the first time. This is often defensive and raw. When newcomers see that there are like minded people in the club their defences are let down and a bond akin to a family bond is likely to be formed. Assumptions are made about the possibilities of mutual aid, common experiences, ideology and how to handle problems arising from the outside world. While these assumptions can turn out to be just that, assumptions rather than fact, there is enough truth to communality to make many quickly feel at home. These bonds are further strengthened by the invitational nature of the club allowing a member to chose not to come to the club at any time for any reason. This means, to some extent, that those who come are self selecting and have a stake in making the club a place where they like to come. This, in turn, drives forward their commitment to the community.

These three aspects, invitational, learning and community, are vital components of the club giving rise to three more guiding principles of the organisation which validate self-determination, continual learning and community in its structure and through the relationships formed at the club.

This most importantly means that each member is responsible for themselves and their learning in any setting. This extends to the activities instigated by the club. There is an organiser but it is up to the members of the community to propose what they would like to see happen and to implement it. While this is very difficult to maintain in a world where people are given very little responsibility for themselves and where we tend to look to others to either tell us what to do or to blame, the taking of responsibility for oneself and one's family is also an empowering position and acts as an incentive to further autonomous relationships.

Another shared principle at club is that children are more equal than adults. This is partly to do with children's literal size but also helps to mitigate (in a small way) the fact that children are treated unequally in the rest of society. To counterbalance this a little, at the club, they are heard, valued, and respected.

The last shared principle is a new definition of 'success'. Success is not defined in terms of exams or wealth or individual happiness but is derived from living according to the guiding principles of the club.   Hopefully this will result in a self confident sense of self and in flexible and negotiable relationships with others.

Putting these principles into practice is difficult. Part of the way this is achieved is through the decision making structures of the club which involves participatory democracy of all members (including children) enabling self determination on both the collective as well as the individual level. This is implemented through constant talking, listening and responding to what is being said. This also involves recognising that things can change from moment to moment depending on factors like age, moods, weather and how many and what mixture of people are at club that day. Moods and weather may sound trivial but in a weekly group of this size they are very important. For example there is an overall year-long mood that changes with the seasons. Attendance of members is usually highest from November through March with the most restless meetings, often leading to some aggressive behaviours, at the end of March. This could be due to the large numbers of members having been cooped up together all winter. After March members begin to look forward to their various summer projects and the mood shifts.

A corollary of participatory democracy is decision making through consensus rather than voting. The club has no formal meetings although there is a place on the timetable for them. This may seem contradictory. Over the years it has been found that meetings are not a good way of problem solving as some people are too shy to speak in front of others or do not have an opinion about the issues raised. It is also possible for some members to dominate meetings and thereby nullify consensus. Children can find meetings boring and rarely, if ever, attend them despite encouragement from the adults. Instead the club has informal delegations of both adults and children that emerge when there is a problem. These groups change and shift depending on what the problem is. Ideas are discussed around the club in small informal groups until a consensus is reached regarding a solution, or there is a shift in attitude which makes the original problem melt away.

In addition, the club is overseen by a benevolent dictator which again appears to contradict the principle of participatory democracy and consensus decision making. But the benevolent dictator is active only to safeguard the over all vision of the club, to maintain participatory democracy and consensus decision making and to further the processes that help the club remain as true to its principles as possible. The 'dictatorship' also adds continuity over the years as families come and go.

It is important that these principles not be explicitly articulated so that newcomers discover them for themselves. This is part of the process of taking responsibility for oneself. The principles are tacitly accepted when families join the club and sometimes it is a long time before people realise what the principles are. Sometimes members never become conscious of the underlying principles, but even these members are able to adapt to them in practise without any problems. Other members are articulate about these principles but have difficulty with one or other of them when it comes to putting them into practice.

While reference is made to learning in the title of this article, there is no mention of education there or in these principles or in the club's ethos. Learning is taken here to be integral and continuous aspect of human life; 'education' has become a constructed specialised activity which can be given and taken away. It functions as an economic category when it is given a 'value' and 'sold' to the individual in the form of an 'expert', or a paid professional that the individual thinks necessary in order to learn. The club is trying to redress this situation by not specifically setting itself up as an educational institution. (The important exception to this is when we have to deal with mainstream society such as in our Articles and Memorandum for being a charity where we have to define ourselves according to given parameters strictly led by conventional thought.)

The size of the club is vital. There is no optimal number for how big or small a club should be to operate effectively but if it is too big it takes more time for members to get to know each other and thereby build a community and if it is too small there may not be enough social interactions for members to feel satisfied. It should be big enough to provide a variety of relationships and small enough for frequent and intimate interactions.

Concluding Remarks

This structure sketched out here is very fragile, changeable and continually bombarded both externally from pressures of mainstream society but, more surprisingly, also internally from the adult members' psychic mechanisms which have been formed by mainstream society. So, for example, even a parent who has been successfully using a child-led learning approach for many years and has a thriving, healthy child will regularly need reassurance that this approach is right for them. Going against the mainstream can be arduous to maintain and often parents who have been happy with alternative styles of development when their children were young start to question their decision when their children reach the age at which they would take exams if they had attended school.

This article began by saying that each invitational learning community is unique and that therefore the experiences of any one particular community cannot be a template for another community. However, through describing a particular successful experience of running an invitational learning centre some general guiding principles were unearthed which could potentially be useful to those starting their own organisation. Hopefully, specifying these principles could also contribute to debates about different types of learning and different forms of community. Further, it is hoped that having knowledge of some underlying principles of procedure will give confidence to those thinking about this endeavour. Although every community will be unique it will also make an important contribution as a place to give reality to an alternative vision of learning and community. It is with this in mind that this article is written.

Reference:

Safran, L (2001) "Creativity as 'Mindful' Learning: A case from Learner-Led Home-Based Education" in *Creativity in Education,* edited by Craft, Jeffrey and Leibling, London:Continuum, 2001

Chapter six

Using Self Managed Learning with Young People

by Ian Cunningham

Karl Marx got a few things wrong, but he also got a few things right. One of the latter was his view that it isn't enough to analyse the world. We have to get on and change things. We know what is wrong with much that goes on under the banner of education and it is no longer any use wasting time analysing it or criticising schooling: we have to get on and change things.

I hear teachers and others complain a lot about the impositions of Government agencies on schooling and education. They often insist that there is no choice – they cannot change things. The Government imposes continuous testing of young people, a narrow curriculum and vicious inspections (the 'light touch' inspection is the equivalent of a tap on the head with a sledgehammer). In this respect it is difficult to maintain any notion that, on a collective basis, teaching is a profession.

As a young newcomer to local government I once asked a civil engineer what made him a professional. He replied: *"If my employer was to ask me to build, say, a bridge that I knew would be unsafe I would refuse. Firstly, I base my judgement on scientific and technical knowledge, which has to guide my actions. Secondly, I have a moral duty to the public who, after all, actually pay my salary."*

A proper profession first of all works from the best available knowledge base and refuses to do otherwise. Yet many teachers knowingly impose approaches on students that they know are less than ideal.

Another dimension of a good professional is an ethical code to which they hold dear and see as over-riding the wishes of those less knowledgeable (such as Government officials). Collectively teachers seem less concerned about such ethical issues. Note that my concern here is with the culture and practice of teaching and not about the individual teacher. Many teachers do take a stand for what they know is right. And it is much more possible to do this than many teachers imagine.

The notion that the dictates of the state should over-ride all other considerations is frequently made. However, the defence of obeying the orders of the state was not accepted at the Nuremberg trials after the Second World War – and some people went to the gallows as a result. I appreciate that this analogy may seem over-dramatic – to make my point, it is. However, to undermine young people and give them a poor start in life is a serious issue. Most of the young people that we work with have had such experiences in school. For instance one student was labelled 'stupid' by his primary school teacher and so he, quite rationally, decided that it was not of use to him to engage with the teaching community. As a result he became technically an 'elective mute' – meaning that he never spoke to anyone in school for three years. The boy was not stupid and once out of school was able to progress his learning quite well.

Another example of the teaching culture came up in a meeting with some primary school heads a few years ago. They had just had their annual SATs round. One complained that some of her students had been difficult because they had burst into tears in the test. She said that she had told them off and insisted that they shape up and stop acting like babies. Another head complained that her best student was off with flu so she had had to go round to the girl's house to administer the test there (even though the girl was very ill); the head did not want her overall results to be pulled down by this girl's results being left out.

I could go on – most readers will have their own stories of some of the horrors of what goes on in schools. My challenge, then, is back to Marx – is not the imperative to do something about this? And more analysis of what is wrong and what should be done - without any notion of action - is a continual betrayal of our young people.

Our work

The rest of this chapter is about one modest piece of work to provide a model of what learning for young people can be about. It is not based on arm-chair theorising or abstract critiques but on real practice that has been carefully evaluated. Our programme is not offered as **the answer** but as **an answer** to the problem. However, I would argue that the principles behind our practice are of universal validity and can be applied anywhere (we have worked in places as different as Sweden and Israel introducing our approach).

We established the *South Downs Learning Centre* over five years ago as part of our educational charity, the *Centre for Self Managed Learning*. Some of us had been running Self Managed Learning programmes for adults for over a quarter of a century and we decided to provide opportunities for young people, having realised that much of what we were doing with, for instance, senior leaders in organisations was remedial activity. I found myself working with Boards of companies and public bodies helping them to get on with each other, to be able to think strategically, to be more innovative and to take a broader view of their role in the world. It seemed to me that it would have been better for them to learn this when they were younger. The effects of a supposed good education had often produced leaders who found it difficult to relate well to others and to work out what life is about.

On this latter point I also ran Self Managed Learning groups for Chief Executives and found that mostly they wanted to explore what would be labelled 'personal issues'. For instance, they had discovered that becoming a Chief Executive did not suddenly make life a whole lot better. One complained that he now had two homes, three cars and a third wife – but had not seen his children grow up and wondered if the sacrifices had been worth it. All of this confirms the research that happiness and self fulfilment are not necessarily related to position or income.

The South Downs Learning Centre

The Centre currently operates out of a Victorian house in Brighton. There are 12 students aged 11-15 and they meet every weekday morning. Most of them have had bad experiences in school. All the students enjoy being in an environment where they can be themselves, where there are no classrooms, no imposed curricula, no teachers, no lessons and no tests – but there is lots of support for their learning.

In communicating our ideas for a learning centre that really provided for young people, we put forward the following list to parents:

Some basic ideas that underpin our approach to learning. (NB these are supported by rigorous research).

1. Learning is not just 'head' stuff. We need to learn in all sorts of ways and about all sorts of things. Learning includes some of the things students have already focused on such as playing a musical instrument or being more self confident or taking photographs or caring for others.
2. Setting goals and having a level of control over achieving this is part of creating a happy and fulfilled life. This especially applies to learning activity.
3. We often learn most with and from others. These 'others' are often, for students, not adults but others in the same boat, for example, in the same age range.
4. If we are to work and operate in the 'real world' getting on with others is a key to being human.
5. Relationships are important. In order to have good relationships with others, listening to others is important.
6. If we can make relationships work we have a chance to make communities work. The Learning Centre models an active community where people feel part of something worthwhile.
7. People are all different – and this needs respecting in a learning community.
8. Traditionally education has tried to make people think together and feel separately. The better way is to think separately and feel together. Community only works if we feel connected to others – and in a positive way – whilst respecting differences.
9. Each person needs space to be able to raise what they like in a learning group. And they

need to be listened to and supported by others in the group.

In the last item we mentioned the idea of learning groups. In our work students join a group of six together with at least one adult acting as a learning assistant (they are there to assist students in their learning). Each student creates their own learning programme through discussion in the group and they write that down in a learning agreement. Each learning agreement is unique to that student. However, we encourage them to think about learning goals at three levels – **life goals, career goals** and **current goals**. For instance a student might come up with one **life goal** to have a happy family life. They may then go on to suggest a possible **career** that would provide a good work/life balance. This might then lead them to indicate particular **current goals,** such as the need to get some GCSEs so that they can go on to college.

Most students initially struggle with the idea of planning out what they want to learn. It takes time and patience to give them the opportunity to have these struggles. It can also be a new experience for them to be in a community of equals. We start each week with a community meeting to consider what collective things need planning. This can include organising visits, the use of resources or decisions on who might do cooking this week. The community then breaks into the two learning groups (one for 13-15 year-olds and the other for 11-13 year-olds). In the groups students draft out a timetable for the week (each student is helped to do their own and every student has a different timetable).

Every student gets their own copy of the timetable and a copy is posted on the wall so that everyone can see what others are doing that week. This is important for collective activity. For instance early last term some students were heavily into film making for a few weeks – they wrote the scripts themselves, acted them out and edited the resulting work. They initially had a rough go at things and then they invited in a film maker who was able to work through with them how to create a more polished piece. They needed to learn to work together to achieve this – and their first attempts at this were not successful as they had been schooled in acting as individuals or they had been used to being directed by an adult.

Sometimes it may be that only one person is passionately interested in something but others will join in. This happened where one 12 year-old student became fascinated by criminal behaviour and what made a person a criminal. He downloaded a great deal of material from the internet, read books and watched TV programmes and then created his own PowerPoint presentation on the subject. He also wrote film scripts based on what he had been learning. We then invited in a former probation officer to talk with him and others. About half the community turned up for a discussion that lasted over an hour, with most of the time being taken up with questions from students. These questions ranged over topics around human behaviour in general (the former probation officer is now a psychotherapist so she was able to engage with their wide-ranging questions).

Following this session we arranged a visit to the local police station and most of the students came along. They were able to ask their own questions about police work and about general issues in the community affecting crime. All of them took away something from the visit and in their own terms.

For instance the 12 year-old student decided to explore a career in the police while others gained insights into police work that developed their general awareness of community problems.

I quote this one small example to show that we do not need teachers, classrooms, lessons, testing and an imposed curriculum. Our focus is on how to assist students to learn in whatever way suits them. We are also clear that 'choice' is not about picking from a fixed menu. To continue the food analogy, it is about students creating their own meals (curriculum) and not picking convenience foods off a supermarket shelf (lessons, subjects, etc). This factor is related to the confusion around the difference between customisation and personalisation.

Customisation is where the provider attempts to categorise people and then provide for these different market segments. In education one way this is being done is through a supposed analysis of students' learning styles and then giving them learning experiences that suit their learning style (although the research evidence does not support such generalisations). Another customising mode is streaming by supposed ability. The 11+ examination was, and still is, used to customise by aptitude/ability. Providing choice in subjects to study is another customising mode. None of these approaches are about personalising.

Personalisation is where we focus on assisting the young person to develop as a unique human being – but one who can only do this effectively through relationships with others. Personalising is not individualising, in the sense of isolating each learner to do their own thing. In order for a person to develop as a person they need to engage in dialogue with others about things that matter and through such dialogue to become who they want to be.

Note that I deliberately use the verb 'to be' here. It is not about just knowing things or doing things (and in this latter regard the current Government emphasis on skills is as much a narrowing exercise as is an over-emphasis on book knowledge). Our interest is in how we can assist young people to lead a good life - and 'good' should not be defined by state functionaries, or by us, but has to come from the person exploring with others what that means to them.

We are not, though, in favour of continual planning for tomorrow. Childhood should not be seen as a tiresome period where a person has to go through some unpleasant experiences in order to lead a full and satisfying life at some future date. The problem is that this delayed gratification leads to a continual 'putting off' enjoying life – the classic being where adults work in order to earn enough to retire and start enjoying life (and then finding that it is not like that).

We encourage young people to enjoy life now **and** prepare themselves for what are really unknown futures. It is not about doing one or the other – they need to do both. And this is initially quite challenging for students. Many find it difficult to create this balance at the start and they swing to one side or the other. Sometimes the initial reaction to the freedom of our Centre is for students to focus more on having fun now and doing little about preparing for the future. However, they gradually start to see the value in a balance, often from the dialogues with other young people and adults around them.

I have emphasised dialogue so far without really defining it. One distinction I make is between **dialogue** and **discussion**. **Discussion** is talk about something 'out there'. In the Centre we have discussions like other communities. Groups making films discuss the script, the roles that people will play, the editing of the raw material and so on. However, when we are encouraging students to engage with each other about what they want to learn we need them to open up about themselves, their values and their beliefs. For instance we start a new learning group by each student giving key aspects of their life history so far (and we adults model this by doing the same). We go on to give each person time to talk about things they want to develop and the way that they want to learn. It may seem initially paradoxical but in order to have **dialogue** you first need monologue – you need each person to have time to say who they are and what they want from life and from the Centre. Then students can understand each other and engage with each other as human beings as opposed to just using stereotypical assumptions ('boys are like this, girls are like this', etc).

The kinds of dialogues we encourage are part of the personalising process for the student. Things to note in this are that we as adults engage with students – but we do not impose on them any subject learning. They need to come to their own realisation about what it is they need to learn, but they may need assistance in this – hence our role as learning assistants.

We are also conscious of the role of parents so we work as closely as we can with them. For instance we have a termly meeting with the student, their parent or parents and at least one of the staff team. We may also have regular contact in between such meetings as we are aware that much of the students learning will go on in the home and in other settings. As much as possible we try to integrate the range of learning experiences that students have. One structure we use is to have a template for each student to plan their week which includes spaces for them to write in what they will do in the mornings with us (Monday to Friday), what they will do in the afternoons and evenings away from the Centre and at weekends. We do not impose on them the need to fill out every space (some do, most do not) but we value knowing what they are able to undertake elsewhere – and some of this is the more solitary learning that they may need to do, such as reading and maths.

Conclusion

We call what we do 'Self Managed Learning' as we want to assist learners to manage their own learning. We also want to assist them to become effective self-managers of their own lives.

The notion of self-management itself is growing. For instance in the health arena there is increasing interest in helping people to take more control over their own health – and there is growing evidence that where people do (for instance with chronic pain) they are able to lead better lives as a result. This is only one small example of what is needed.

We are also clear that real self-managing includes other people. We know that good relationships with others around us (ones that are based on real dialogue) are correlated, on average, with increased satisfaction with life and with greater longevity. Self Managed Learning is not about being highly selfish or self-centred – it is about learning in community.

Chapter seven

Connecting Cultures and Learning for Life: The Bridge International Youth Project

by Jackie Rose

Introduction

The *Bridge International Youth Project* is run by North Staffordshire-based B Arts - a pioneering participatory arts organisation that was established in 1985 by Hilary Hughes, Susan Clarke and the late Gill Gill. The organisation works with people of all ages and backgrounds and has a culture of responding to unmet needs. This ethos results in a focus on working with marginalised and disadvantaged groups. They have generated and supported their own groups, and they have also engaged in partnerships with a range of freelance artists and with other groups and organisations from both the statutory and the voluntary sectors. They have engaged in a wealth of diverse and innovative projects in local, national and international settings.

In 2006 the *Creative Communities Unit* at Staffordshire University carried out an evaluation of the *Bridge Project*, funded by the Diana, Princess of Wales Memorial Fund. The author was employed as a researcher to complete the evaluation and report on the findings (Rose & Webster 2007). This chapter is based upon some of the knowledge and insights that were gained through conducting the evaluation; also on a later discussion with B Arts' Co-Director Hilary Hughes, which took place in November 2007 and focused more specifically on the nature of learning at the *Bridge Project*.

The Bridge Project

The idea for the *Bridge Project* was initially conceived back in 2000, when the team at B Arts became aware through their existing work and contacts, of possible unmet needs on the part of young asylum seekers and refugees. The Immigration and Asylum Act (1999) had introduced the policy of dispersing asylum seekers on a no-choice basis from London and the South East of England to other parts of the country. Stoke-on-Trent had been selected as a recipient city. It is not difficult to envisage some of the challenges that might be faced by asylum seekers arriving in unfamiliar areas. It is also clear to see that their arrival in the early days of the dispersal system would have presented many organisations that had little or no prior experience of working with asylum seekers and refugees with a steep learning curve.

In tackling this learning curve themselves, B Arts followed a process familiar to informal educators:

> *"We make an assessment of what may be going on and our role. We engage in conversation. This raises questions. We consider these in relation to what we discern makes for human flourishing. This enables us to develop a response..."*
> Jeffs & Smith (2005:78)

Thus, by 2001, having successfully engaged around a dozen young people through a celebratory meal and a short residential, and having explored the unmet needs of this group, B Arts decided to develop a project designed to engage specifically with asylum seekers and refugees. Since then, the *Bridge Project* has expanded and developed. Membership constantly fluctuates, but at the time of the evaluation included over eighty young people. Members come from a range of different countries and the target age range of the project is 13-25. Some members are unaccompanied minors and the overall majority are male - though all activities are open to female members as well.

Bridge Project Activities

The *Bridge Project* offers members regular drop-in sessions, with opportunities to socialise. This can be seen as a time for fellowship. Jeffs & Smith (2005:41-42) suggest that fellowship is commonly understood as *"a companionship of people on friendly and equal terms"*, and point out that informal education has long focused on fellowship as part of its concern with happiness. It is based on the recognition that we are social beings, and therefore on the importance of our interactions with others. At these drop-ins project staff are also there to provide individual support, advocacy and mentoring. The support is available on a long-term, unconditional basis and it is based entirely on individual needs: these might include homelessness; understanding letters and forms; contacting other agencies, or perhaps help with school or college work. Workers can enable members to learn from the experiences of others by making them aware of relevant knowledge and opportunities: a role very similar to that described by Tony Jeffs and Mark K Smith:

> *"The task of informal educators is not to passively allow people [to] 'learn from their mistakes'. That can be costly. It is, where*

appropriate, to act as a clearing-house, linking people to ideas, theories and knowledge which will serve them well. It is to function as a bridge between the experiences of those who went before and the present. "

Jeffs & Smith (2005:68)

The project also offers a varied range of arts, sports and cultural activities to encourage personal development and social interaction. The arts activities, some of them music-based, can provide people from diverse backgrounds with opportunities for shared creativity and enjoyment. Similarly, sporting activities – from swimming to canoeing to football to cycling - facilitate cross-cultural participation as well as promoting positive and healthy lifestyles. There are various opportunities for engaging with wider communities: members take part in community events, such as carnivals, and they visit other towns and cities, enabling them to explore beyond their immediate environment, thus learning more about the UK. Visits to museums and other cultural attractions add further knowledge about UK life and history. Some of the visits are residentials, and Hilary Hughes describes how even a short residential trip can be immensely valuable in terms of facilitating conversations and developing positive relationships between members and staff. Another important way that many members have been able to meet other people and to develop cross-cultural understandings has been through taking part in a play entitled *'Reading the Book of Freedom'.* The play is based on real-life experiences of Bridge members and has toured many primary schools in Staffordshire, raising awareness of the issues that asylum seekers face and encouraging dialogue between Bridge members and school pupils.

As well as the broad spectrum of learning opportunities, the project acts as a kind of 'pre-college'. Two of the funding streams are driven by 'NEET' agendas (young people not in education, employment or training), and through this, the project enables members to undertake an accredited qualification - the Open College Network *'Creative Communications'* course. This introduces a slightly more formal aspect to the project provision, though Hilary Hughes explains that because they do not currently offer higher than a Level 1 qualification, the tasks involved can be successfully completed within the informal context of the drop-in sessions at the project. In addition to providing valuable structure to the sessions, the qualification offers some accreditation for members who may wish to go on to study at college.

Project workers actively encourage members to further their formal education, and offer support to members who are studying. Through the project activities, there is extra support for language and literacy development, and ICT skills. In addition, a programme of citizenship education is incorporated into the drop-in sessions. This is designed to help members to adapt to life in the UK, and to better understand the cultural differences that exist. The programme has included a huge range of topics, including differences between schools in different countries; road safety and insurance; the environment, and different food and eating customs (to name just a few examples).

Outreach and detached work also takes place, which aims to ensure inclusiveness and is vital to the many potential members who might not be familiar with the practice of youth work, and therefore may not easily understand what is on offer at the project. People's involvement is facilitated by the fact that all activities are totally free to members, and staff work to address any barriers to participation.

Diversity and personalised learning

No-one who is eligible to join the *Bridge Project* is turned away, even though many arrive with complex needs. The inclusive approach generates diversity, and this is seen at the *Bridge Project* in terms of people's age, nationality, language, experiences and in terms of the particular issues that they may face. The diversity very much invites personalised approaches to learning (see *Personalised Education Now*: no date). Learning at the *Bridge Project* is invitational: there is no formal commitment to attend; no pressure to take part in particular activities; members can do as much or as little as they like and are thus able to progress at their own speed. This informality presents particular challenges for the organisation. Membership fluctuates - often linked to events in other parts of the world. During times of significant increases in membership, the commitment to providing one-to-one support that is not time-limited, clearly makes it very challenging for staff to continue delivering the extensive programme of project activities. Numbers of people attending are unpredictable; people may not turn up to planned activities, and even if they do, they may struggle to make any sort of commitment due to the nature of their lives. This again clearly makes planning provision extremely difficult.

As well as these practical issues in relation to planning, there is a significant tension in relation to providing learning opportunities and encouraging people to think ahead and to plan, when many face uncertain futures over which they have little control. As Hilary Hughes explains:

"There's a very interesting tension between what's happening to them out there in the world and what educators are trying to do with them. And sometimes they can't take it that seriously because they're going 'well how do I know what's going to happen to me?'"

One of the ways in which the project team deals with this is to provide regular annual events at particular times of the year to offer people a kind of structure that they can 'fall in and out of'. They also deal with it by trying to keep the approaches to learning at the project firmly rooted in the realities of people's lives. This involves both actively involving members themselves in developing the project provision, and also taking a very broad view of learning and recognising the value of apparently modest achievements. In doing so, they put into practice two of the key ethical values that are associated with personalised education: a commitment to democratic approaches and the re-integration of learning, life and community.

Democratic approaches at the Bridge Project

It is of great significance that B Arts engaged with refugees and asylum seekers at a very early stage following the introduction of dispersal to North Staffordshire. From the outset, they sought to get people actively involved in developing the services *that they wanted and needed.* Furthermore, the employment of refugees as project workers is one of the key aspects of the *Bridge Project*: three members of staff at B Arts are themselves refugees, two of whom are employed specifically to work with the *Bridge Project*. This approach offers a range of advantages to the members, including overcoming some language barriers and the sharing of cultural customs. That the workers will have first-hand experience of many of the problems faced by project members, means they can also act as role models. The approach requires considerable commitment by the workers and the organisation as a whole. Workers are taking on what is a challenging role under any circumstances, and there are clearly extra difficulties involved for someone from a different culture and whose first language is not English. Sustained levels of training and support are vital. According to Hilary Hughes, it is the *combination* of the knowledge and experience of the project workers from other countries with that of the British workers that has been found at the *Bridge Project* to be the most successful approach in terms of developing cross-cultural understandings and helping people adapt to UK life. In addition to the paid workers, volunteering by older members and sometimes ex-members is also encouraged at the drop-in sessions and on activities and residential trips. This contributes to the apparent overall culture of mutual support at the project.

Meighan (2005:38) suggests that within democratic learning systems *"dialogue becomes an essential activity rather than an optional feature"*, and he highlights the importance of 'purposive conversation' as a learning method. Conversation is a fundamental part of the practice within the *Bridge Project*. Not only is it recognised as being valuable in itself, but it also forms the basis of much of the learning. This includes helping members to identify their learning priorities, and to work out how they might achieve them. Hilary Hughes outlines how this can actually work in practice:

> *"On Friday I'm going to go in and do drumming. What will happen is I'll talk to people, and I'm always looking for the point at which they show me anything that they want to do, or that they want to learn, or something that they need to*

understand. You don't say to them that that's what you're looking for... but in a way those conversations can be quite guided. They can be really quite focused."

It is particularly difficult to negotiate a curriculum at the project, especially with newer members, because of their limited understanding of what may actually be available. Hughes argues that for this reason people will rarely suggest a particular activity: rather, members are encouraged to take part in a range of project activities on a 'try it and see' basis:

"Having once seen it, having once tasted it, having once experienced it they can go 'now I want that again', so that's where the negotiation comes- 'we want to repeat that'. You can't negotiate about something when you have no menu, when you have no idea at all of what the possibilities are. So the negotiations are sometimes about 'try this from those sets of things and then we'll choose from those sets of things'. So we have to drive the choice."

Members are able to express their views through regular planning and review sessions. Awareness of the need to encourage the young people to try new things that challenge their comfort zones and show them where the wider possibilities might lie, along with the frequent changes to the membership of the project, leads to an on-going and dynamic quest for new learning activities.

Re-integration of learning, life and community

The principle of re-integrating learning, life and community is translated into practice at the *Bridge Project* in more ways than can be mentioned here. It can be seen in the many ways that the project works to help members adapt to life in the UK, including the programme of citizenship education and the trips out and about. It can be seen in the ways that social activities such as shared meals are seen also as opportunities to informally educate members about food hygiene and healthy eating. It can also be very clearly seen in the huge emphasis on supporting people with their most real and pressing concerns. This very broad view of learning is what leads John Holt (2004) to write about 'doing' or 'doing things better' as opposed to 'learning', as he suggests that learning can imply something that is separate from the rest of life:

"The trouble with talk about 'learning experiences' is that it implies that all experiences can be divided into two kinds, those from which we learn something, and those from which we learn nothing. But there are no experiences from which we learn nothing. We learn something from everything we do, and everything that happens to us or is done to us..."

He argues that what we learn will depend on the experience and how we feel about it, and that the learning may have positive or negative impacts - and adds that:

*"... we are very unlikely to learn anything good from experiences which do not seem **to us** closely connected with what is interesting and important in the rest of our lives. Curiosity is never idle; it grows out of real concerns and real needs. "* [Emphasis in original]

Holt (2004:12)

In helping people to address their real concerns and needs, the emphasis at the *Bridge Project* is very much on showing people how to do something, as opposed to doing it for them. This may involve something as simple as teaching someone how to use a telephone directory as opposed to just looking up the number for them. In the environment of the *Bridge Project*, there is recognition of the significance of learning achievements that in other contexts might seem relatively minor. It is important to remember that for members to find out about the *Bridge Project* – to make a bus trip to get there and to turn up on time for activities that they want to take part in - all involves learning experiences in the broadest sense. Indeed, some members in the most difficult circumstances may be primarily coming along to the project for warmth and food, and they may not wish to extend their learning involvement beyond these initial steps. As with the principles of personalised education, learning at the *Bridge Project* is linked to readiness; no assessments are imposed, so it is accepted that the extent to which people engage with the available learning opportunities will vary immensely.

The result of combining democratic approaches to learning with a focus on re-integrating learning, life and community is a project where members are far from being passive recipients of education. Instead, there is a relationship of learning at the *Bridge Project* which involves project members, staff, and other people who have contact with the project. Individuals engage with each other, and learn together and from each other. It is a kind of learning that is frequently unpredictable and that people are generally unlikely to consciously recognise or identify as new knowledge or understanding. We have seen the very broad range of learning that can be related to the *Bridge Project:* some of which relates to people's most serious concerns; some of which may help them to further their education, and some of which is mainly about trying new experiences and learning new skills - but would probably be viewed by most members as simply having a good time doing fun activities in the company of friends.

References

Holt, J. (2004) *Instead of Education: Ways to Help People Do Things Better (2nd Edition)*, Boulder: Sentient Publications

Jeffs, T. Smith, M.K. (2005) *Informal Education-conversation, democracy and learning (3rd Edition)*, Nottingham: Educational Heretics Press.

Meighan, R. (2005) *Comparing Learning Systems: the good, the bad, the ugly and the counter-productive,* Nottingham: Educational Heretics Press.

Personalised Education Now (no date) **Principles of Personalisation.** Nottingham, Personalised Education Now. Available from: <http://c.person.ed.gn.apc.org> [Accessed 6 December 2007]

Rose, J. Webster, M. (2007) *The Bridge International Youth Project Evaluation,* Stoke-on-Trent: Staffordshire University.

Acknowledgements

I would like to thank Aram Karem, of B Arts, for his contribution in co-leading a workshop at the *Personalised Learning: Taking Choice Seriously Conference* at Staffordshire University in June 2007. I would also like to thank Hilary Hughes for her participation in the development of this chapter.

Chapter eight

Rethinking the Principles of Personalisation and the Role of Digital Technologies

by Tim Rudd

Introduction

Earlier this decade, the concept of personalisation was brought into broad educational parlance strongly supported by some key researchers and the Government, largely whilst David Milliband was Minister of State for School Standards. In his speech at the North of England Education Conference (Miliband 2004a) he stated that the way to better standards in education *"was to focus not on what we teach but on how we teach"* with there being greater choice and voice for pupils within the education system and that personalisation would lead to systemic change. The logic behind the need for a change in the education system was underpinned by a broader thesis of industrial production put forward by Piore and Sabel (1990). In this thesis the argument was that the era of mass production had been replaced by one of 'flexible specialisation'. Rather than a system based on mass production and limited choice, consumers now have far greater choice in terms of products and services that are in keeping with their personal needs and requirements. This has meant a move away from Fordist methods of mass production and Taylorist principles, to ones of higher flexibility and ability to respond to consumer needs. The suggestion was that schools were still in the mass production stage and need to change in order to offer an educational approach that enabled similar levels of diversity.

Drawing on these broad arguments, it is implied that for learning and teaching to become more personalised there needed to be more choice for pupils and less rigidity both in pre-defined curriculum content and teaching methods and approaches, taking into account learners individuals learning needs and interests. The argument also implied that in producing a more 'flexibly specialised' educational approach, some of the systemic inequalities that arise from a competitive system based on a 'one size fits all' approach to formal learning might be overcome.

Miliband (2004b) argued there were five key components of personalised learning, namely: understanding strengths and weaknesses of individual pupils; developing confidence and competences of each learner based on individual needs; curriculum choice that engages and respects students; radical approaches to school organisation; and the community, local institutions and social services supporting schools to drive progress forward in classrooms. However, whilst these key components provided an interesting route map or starting point for the development of personalised education, progress has remained relatively slow as many of the existing political imperatives continue to somewhat negate any significant widespread systemic reforms. Moreover, a lack of further or clearer exemplification of the principles underpinning personalisation still persists. Limited further theoretical and philosophical input around the concept from the Government, and what this means in terms of implications for teaching and learning, relationships between pupils and teachers, and the broader competencies we hope children will learn in order for them to develop the kinds of learning dispositions needed for the 21st century, remain under-explored. As a result, the concept of personalisation is often used in a tokenistic manner, as a 'buzz word' and perhaps even as shorthand to legitimise decisions, activities and products that do not really promote a personalised approach to education.

Another key issue relating to the limited debate and development of the concept in educational terms is that in using Piore and Sabel's thesis, the theoretical arguments may have already been based on an outdated vision, and also one that was not necessarily appropriate to education and harnessing the new digital tools available. It may be argued that whilst their thesis presented an excellent theory around changes in the methods of production and consumerism, further changes over the last decade and a half have further placed the potential for production and creation of materials in the hands of the 'consumer' and moreover have gifted people the tools to represent their identities in various ways unfathomable to most of us in 1990. Rather than a move from mass production of limited goods toward more choice over the range of products to purchase, use and incorporate in our daily lives, we are now moving to an era whereby increasingly individuals can virtually choose, design and assemble the products and services for themselves. Granted, this is still some way off in many areas of daily life, yet increasingly we are seeing possibilities for individuals to have greater control over the development of their own 'products'. Nowhere is this more visible than in relation to new digital technologies where individuals can create their own resources, place them for the whole world to see, should they choose to do so, share them, contribute to and edit others materials and even send or sell these to other individuals or communities across traditional geographical and demographic boundaries. A broader 'network logic' (McCarthey *et al.* 2004) that is permeating society is demanding new skills and dispositions, yet this is very often at odds with the methods and tools of instruction and the relatively isolated and contained nature of learning within schools.

So, whilst the Government still continues to drive forward to a more personalised education system through a range of initiatives, including its 'Harnessing Technology' strategy and related programmes, it is essential that the underlying *principles of personalisation* are re-examined, so that the logic of the education system is altered to place learners as active subjects at the centre of learning rather than as objects navigating the needs of a system incorporating rigid measures and methods of assessment, pre-defined curricula, passive and abstract learning methods. The changes that are being implied by moving to a truly personalised education system are dependent on innovation occurring within compulsory, formal education, both in terms of the utilisation of new technologies (to date largely used as a delivery mechanism to help meet the needs of existing curricula) but perhaps more importantly, in approaches to learning and teaching.

The remainder of this paper seeks to outline and debate some of the key principles of personalisation and argue why these should be at the heart of future considerations and developments. It also attempts to illustrate how new digital technologies might enable a more personalised approach to learning by offering greater economy of scale, diversity and potential to create, share and edit content than was previously possible and place learners in greater control over the learning process.

Re-examining notions of learner choice

Firstly, let us return to the notion of choice which has been stated as one of the central tenets underpinning personalisation. To begin with, for the most part children do not have choice over whether or not they actually attend school or indeed which school they will go to. Their power to choose or select alternatives is removed, by proxy, or at best severely limited. Whilst it is unlikely that the vast majority of the population would have this any other way, this may be seen as the very beginnings of the development of a hierarchical set of structured relationships that develops early on between learners, teachers and school and which may, therefore, be a basis for the beginning of a process of acculturation into a passive mode of learning. Unless action is taken within schools to empower learners, they will learn to be, or rather learn it is wrong not to be, largely passive recipients or consumers of pre-defined and externally imposed content rather than active creators of it.

Most learners are aware of the potential many digital technologies offer them to become active creators of materials outside of compulsory educational setting. Increasingly learners are familiar with seeking out, or at least the possibility of seeking out, joining and participating in communities with others with similar interests, and contributing to debates and actively influencing the form and content of these. They are familiar with the notion of developing online identities, the notion that material is to be shared for collective benefit, with being able to create new materials, online identities, reputations and how and when contributions are effective. Whilst much of this would not be perceived to be formal learning, many have an understanding or the building blocks to develop skills that could be utilised in the development of their own learning pathways. However, the formal education system does not appear keen draw on this, to build upon or develop these abilities and to incorporate these skills and harness them to support learners formal learning. Schools often operate as *learned* ones where a largely one way transmission of knowledge occurs as learners come to consume set knowledge deemed as 'ideal' or exemplary, rather than being *learning* institutions based on mutli-way development of knowledge utilising all available resources.

A second issue around choice is whether learners have any real choice over *what they learn*? Are not curricula usually largely pre-defined for them? In relation to personalisation, the vast majority of discussions around choice to date have tended to focus to date around different ways of navigating existing curricula or increasing options available rather than being about real alternatives, ways in which learners might develop their own choices, how to foster their abilities to choose and develop their own ways of creating their own learning pathways. As such, learners might have more options but this does not necessarily represent any *real choice*.

Clearly there are many times and areas of learning when passive learning and didactic teaching are the most effective and fruitful methods but ironically, such approaches appear to become more prevalent the longer a learner spends in the compulsory education, as their potential ability to understand and express their learning needs and interests actually increase. This is largely driven by assessment and standards criteria which become increasingly intense in the secondary phase and limit the diversity and choice available to learners. This also increases the likelihood that learning and teaching becomes focused on 'consuming' factual content for the purpose of examination and negates the potential for teaching or supporting the development of some of the broader and more transferable competencies and skills that may be more applicable to the lives of learners in the 21st century. Returning to the notion of personalisation therefore, can we really see a significant move to greater consumer, or rather learner choice, without significant changes in the current modes of assessment and the common standards agenda that underpins and shapes them? Without significant change and innovation the plausibility of developing personalised individual learning pathways and diverse curricula will be significantly limited, and therefore the choices needed to deliver a truly personalised education system will remain unattainable.

Outside of formal education, developments in new technologies have provided the basis for more diversity and learning on a massive scale and many learners are already familiar with these techno-cultural tools and the possibilities they can bring. In relation to learning, new technologies enhance the potential to investigate new areas, to engage in synchronous and asynchronous communications with experts or people with similar interests, to create content and share it with others in through a range of media, to share others material, add to and edit it and work with others across geographical and traditional age-stage boundaries. The tools for diversity exist, but the will to harness these to provide extensive learning choices for learners is still some way off in most formal compulsory contexts, although pockets of practice to develop. Providing diversity of choice at a systemic level will require 'harnessing' technology as a transformational tool to deliver a truly personalised vision and not, as has often been the case, subverting and under-utilising the technology for the requirements of an existing and outmoded system.

A further related issue is the basis for choosing and developing learning content. There are many different ways that skilled educators can direct learners but many teachers feel restricted by the demands of a delivery focused system to take the necessary 'risks' to allow them to experiment with different approaches. Alternative methods of developing learner driven and emergent curricula are sometimes messy, difficult to assess, and their dynamic can make short and medium term planning extremely difficult. Moreover, much teacher training and development still focuses on methods to deliver the existing system requirements and if a move to a personalised approach is to be pursued, this training must focus specifically on the personalised alternatives to existing practice. If, we are to deliver a customised approach to education suited to the interests and needs of learners and offer a 'choice of curriculum that respects students' do we not need to think about more emergent learning, one that has at its centre, and builds upon, the interests, existing abilities and needs of learners.

Luis Moll et al. (1992; 2005) promote a much more culturally responsive, ethnographic approach to teaching and learning. Taking an enquiry-based approach to understanding learners existing skills, interests, abilities and home and community resources, teachers adapt their teaching styles and develop appropriate learning experiences and resources. Moreover, in taking this approach they mobilise the wider resources available in local communities and by mapping out and analysing learner skills and experiences, learners and teachers become funds of knowledge for one another, thereby challenging existing relationships and approaches to learning. Moreover, this approach has a positive psychological and empowering impact on learners, signifying that formal learning is customised around them and draws on culturally relevant aspects of their lives as a basis for developing diverse, personalised learning pathways.

New technologies now exist that can theoretically support such approaches in a more scalable way. It is relatively easy with the right approach to provide learners with the tools to capture their own interests and resources, for example, through digital audio, still image or video. There are online spaces where these can be uploaded and tagged if desired by themselves, other learners and teachers if required. Learning conversation can then take place about the best ways to harness these resources in support of their formal learning, competency and skills development, or perhaps how formal learning might better support their outside interests. Once areas of interest are identified educators can support learners to become more information literate, find sources of knowledge, others interested in the same area or similar subjects with whom they might communicate or work, appropriate areas to post or share their work, and other experts in a particular field who may guide or offer them inspiration. The role of the educator necessarily moves toward one of mentor and guide to support the development of a positive learning disposition through negotiated approaches to customised curriculum development.

Other software that is in development is being specifically developed that aims to put the learner at the centre of the development of customised learning from the outset. The My-E (My Education) prototype, for example, is being developed by *Futurelab* and aims to help very young learners develop meaningful conversations that are supported in both the home and the school with the purpose of trying to make home cultures and learner interests more visible. These 'conversations' can be stored, edited and embellished with video, audio and still images and then tagged and stored. Whilst this is only a prototype at this stage, it does demonstrate how new technologies can be harnessed to support more learner focused and empowering learning experiences. However, to move to a more personalised approach requires a broader understanding of the practices required to really 'develop the confidence and competences of each learner based on individual needs'. A range of flexible and multi-functional digital tools exist (such as content repositories and e-portfolios) that enable a form of customisation in relation to learning content, data storage and analysis functions. Again, however, the control of many of these tools that purport to help support a more personalised approach remain largely in the hands of those 'guardians of the system' and their main use is often to monitor the behaviour and learning of pupils in relation to top down systemic requirements rather than real learner needs. Often, this is reflected in the design and specific functionality of such tools, however, it not beyond the realms of possibility that many of these powerful resources could be designed to specifically reflect learner driven needs and interests with educators taking a more responsive role as a result. Many educational technologies are developed to support existing market needs and as a result their functionality mirrors the needs of the existing system. It was surely no coincidence that

Interactive Whiteboards, for example were developed to be placed at the front of the classroom, where the traditional blackboard might have been, and in the hands of the teacher demonstrating and relaying information to a classroom of thirty or so pupils. Despite the potential functionality, any interactivity that occurs is therefore mediated by the teacher. The same or similar technology could have (and now has) been designed to be embedded in tables to promote more collaboration amongst small groups of pupils thereby actually increasing the likelihood of greater interactivity. This is just one example of many, but we must beware of the gloss and hype that surrounds new technologies as tools for delivering personalisation, are negated and mediated by existing practices.

A third and related issue around choice is around *when* pupils learn. There are many aspect to this but perhaps one of the main ones surrounds established age-stage boundaries. Learners engage with learning content and assessed on how well they are adjudged to deal with it, not only in relation to their immediate peers but also to the whole formal school or age cohort. This is perceived as a method for assessing standards across the system but actually overlooks what is known about developing effective learning positions. Yes, learners need to be challenged but children develop at different rates and often have a broad range of skills, experiences and abilities that should provide the basis for diverse and specialised learning approaches and experiences. Most learners choices are severely limited by having to engage with set content at the same time and effectively in 'competition' with huge numbers of other pupils because of the measurement and testing systems in operation. This can have potentially damaging effects that arise from the internalised perceptions of learners about their abilities that can have long lasting effects. It may be argued that this is not a system that 'understands the strengths and weaknesses of pupils', but rather one that looks for weakness set against somewhat rigid and arbitrarily imposed criteria. If a personalised system is to be delivered, broad snapshot measures will have to be re-thought and replaced by ones that support and scaffold the learners broader development.

The issue of where children learn is also one that warrants much greater attention, especially in light of both new technological developments and large capital development initiatives, such as the £45 billion *Building Schools for the Future* programme, which aims to rebuild or remodel every secondary school in England, and therefore presents a once in a generation opportunity to rethink possibilities and develop built pedagogy suited to the 21st century. Combined intelligently to push the boundaries and deliver personalised education, these could really lead to the 'radical approaches to school organisation' that were heralded by the Labour Government. Do learners all have to attend the same school, the same lessons, at the same time? If we are to move to a truly customised set of learner led curricula, is this really practical or appropriate? Re-thinking the notion of learning spaces, away from the 'institutional logic' that prevails offers many opportunities for organising learning differently. For example, is there the potential to build 'learning hubs' or satellites that could allow learners to go into specialist learning spaces, whether these were organised based on particular skills or in subject fields, or perhaps they could be there to support where a learner is in any stage of a creative learning project. This is just one speculative example, but it does not take too much imagination to see how learning might be organised differently; how different learners may take on different roles; how age-stage barriers might be more readily removed (not only in terms of compulsory age learners); how different places might be alternatively resourced; and how learners utilise spaces set up more specifically to support their needs. If we are to offer the diversity and specialisms required to promote personalised learning then linking in with and drawing on the expertise, needs and funds of knowledge that exist in broader communities (real and virtual) is essential. Only in creating more diverse arrangements are we really likely to see 'the community, local institutions and social services supporting learning and driving progress forward'.

A fourth and related issue around choice is that of who learners actually learn with. Deep personalisation, or broad customisation is unlikely to be delivered consistently by one teacher and possibly a classroom assistant when there are around thirty pupils in a classroom. To offer the kinds of diversity required to enable learners to create their own specific learning pathways, we have to consider arrangements with wider communities and individuals, such as those outlined above, as well as considering different ways of utilising experts or co-learners from a range of different locations. New technologies make this possible, if even remotely... Video and tele-conferencing are now accessible and in some cases free, as is the possibility of working with others from a range of potential contexts, ages and varied roles and having a shared 'space' to place learning resources, discuss issues, find others to work with and so forth.

Reconsidering learner voice

Again, the term learner voice has permeated educational discourse in recent years, and was a heralded as a central concept to support the Governments move toward personalisation. However, again this has suffered from the necessary philosophical and theoretical discussions and analysis of what this means in practice. Once it became embedded in wider political and educational discourse, it soon gained 'value' but simultaneously became to be used tokenistically and unproblematically in reference to anything that intimated asking learners their opinions on any subject or issues, whether learners themselves were actively involved, whether they had any influence on the debates, agenda, the methods and motives for engagement, or what happens as a result of any feedback they might offer. Clearly projects and activities labelled as 'learner voice' are often not empowering to the learner, do not develop those broader skills relating to debate, negotiation, organisation, agenda setting and planning and ultimately are not empowering. The ultimate aim of deep and empowering learner voice activities is to mobilise and develop learners as pro-active members of communities in which their input and influence can have a direct effect on the form, function, processes and practices of that community.

Erickson and Schultz (1992) argue that learner or pupil voice activities and projects should be about enabling learners to develop critical awareness of their own abilities, methods and capacities for learning but note that the structure and organisation of school negates the possibility of learner's voices being fostered to any great extent. The ability for learners to be involved in real and active participation as part of a learning community, tends to be hampered by the structural and political requirements and the relatively isolated way in which schools operate. Of course, involvement and the extent of learner voice activities vary across schools and different aspects of school life but it is certainly far from a central tenet of teaching and learning approaches.

Drawing on Arnstein's 'ladder of participation' (1969) relating to community involvement and participation, eight 'rungs' of participation, which are broadly divided into three levels of engagement can be identified. These might be used as a basis for considering and analysis the extent to which learners voices are heard in schools. The first level of engagement that Arnstein describes is that of *non-participation* (made up of three 'rungs' - 'manipulation', 'decoration' and 'informing') and can generally be categorised by non-participation by individuals, a lack of information of their rights, non communication of decisions made and the reasons underpinning them, and at best the rubber stamping of decisions that have already been made. The next level is that of *tokenism* (made up of the three 'rungs' - 'consultation', 'placation' and 'partnership'). In this level there is greater involvement with individuals being informed, encouraged to express their opinions and negotiation over outcomes. Many would argue that this represents the voice of the individual but the issue of who sets agendas is still debatable. If we are to develop the types of skills, competencies and abilities for learners to fully participate, we may need to take another step toward the third level, that which Arnstein describes as *empowerment* (made up of two rungs - 'delegated power' and 'control'). At this level, the individual or community actively sets agenda, decides on the issues of importance, the best way to debate them and take action toward resolutions and developments.

For a truly personalised approach to education, not only do educators and policy makers have to re-visit and re-examine notions of voice and choice and think what these really mean in a personalised educational future, but they also have to consider how to find the time, space and opportunities to innovate and to enable the learners to develop the associated skills, alongside the following:

Creating responsible and (pro)active learners

Responsibility is often equated with aspects of what is deemed as acceptable or good behaviour in pupils but this is not what is at issue here necessarily. What is more essential are the opportunities, abilities and scaffolding in place to enable learners to grow in confidence and learn the processes and practices needed for them to take greater control and shape their own learning, negotiating and setting their own goals and agendas, enabling them to plan, search, resource, communicate and collaborate with a wide range of others to support their learning aims. This should be the a fundamental aspect of 21st century learning.

Creativity, problem solving and 'content' creation

Creativity is not only rewarding but has core skills that can be applied to a range of different contexts. Whilst creativity and innovation can be developed to a degree through theoretical and abstracted practice, this is of limited use without putting things into practice. Similarly, deep learning is more likely through real projects with tangible results, where learners get to demonstrate their creativity through development of new artefacts or resources, where there is an audience and where they are likely to give feedback on outputs. There are now numerous digital tools that allow learners to do exactly that, to learn through design, to create materials and try out new tools, developing skills and talents and to learn from others with similar aims and challenges.

Communication

Communication skills are often cited as a core skill for learners, but how do we expect to develop this in learners unless we place them in greater control over learning processes, to enable them to debate and discuss with others, to try approaches and methods of participation, to learn negotiation and influencing skills and ways of conveying information and ideas? Can our formal education system really encourage the development of such skills in any great degree when there are so many targets that need to be met, or is there insufficient time and room in the system to fully develop these and also the various mechanisms and media through which they can be enhanced.

Collaboration

Despite the developing network logic emerging in society, schools operate as relatively isolated institutions. Surely there is a need to look at various ways and possibilities for encouraging learners to collaborate with others as a core ability. New digital tools offer people more ways to collaborate then ever before and learners need to practice the skills for collaboration and also utilise the full range of tools on offer and to make them aware of the means by which it may occur. This is at odds with the 'walled garden' approaches that tend to dominate the schools sector and represents an under-utilisation of excellent resources.

Digital literacy and multi-modal learning

If the vast array of tools and resources that can help learners customise their approach and area of study, more in keeping with their interests, needs and abilities are to be mobilised effectively, there is a need to develop a much broader understanding of the varied types of digital literacies and approaches to learning that exist and are developing. Many of these challenge more traditional views on ways and methods for learning. It is important to understand these, realise their overall value to different aspects of learning and to understand that use of media have different yet equally valid forms of engagement and operation.

Conclusion

Whilst there is much talk about personalisation, broader public debates about what it is, how it might manifest itself, how it will and should change the relationships between learners and teachers and learners and learners, how it will change the organisation and activities in schools, and how curricula, measurement and assessment systems will have to change if real change is to be delivered, have all to be re-visited and critically re-examined. Numerous changes have occurred but without clearer exemplification of the model of personalisation, many educators will remain confused, tokenistic interpretations will remain unchallenged and opportunities to move practice and policy forward will be missed. It is time to re-visit the concept on a national scale and create the demand for systemic change to ensure we improve and deliver and more relevant and valid education system for the 21st century.

It is clear that significant changes in the short term are likely to remain incremental at best, however, the concept of personalisation might be seen as existing along a continuum and as long as there is a constant and visible move toward the deeper forms, then there is hope of significant longer term reform. However, there is equally the chance that without exploring the concept further and gaining a better understanding of the changes required, the skills to be fostered and the changes in teaching practice necessary, that the concept will wither as a powerful tool for systemic reform.

New technologies offer new ways of offering the diversity, flexibility and scalability to support the delivery of multifarious individual learning pathways on an unprecedented scale. However, schools are still unwilling or unable to fully harness their potential in this way and to deliver a personalised approach at a system wide level, such tools need to be appropriated, not as delivery mechanisms for an outdated and outmoded system but as a means to diversify, connect and challenge existing perceptions of what, where and how learning takes place.

References

Miliband, D. (2004a) 'Personalised Learning: Building A New Relationship With Schools'. Speech by David Miliband at the *North of England Education Conference, Belfast. January 8th*.

Miliband, D. (2004b) *Choice and Voice in Personalised Learning*. Accessed (03/01/08) http://www.oecd.org/dataoecd/58/36/39113236.doc

Sabel, P. and Piore, M. (1990) *The Second Industrial Divide: Possibilities for Prosperity*, Basic Books: United States

DfES (2005) *Harnessing Technology: Transforming learning and children's services*. Accessed (03/01/08). http://www.dfes.gov.uk/publications/e-strategy

McCarthy, H. Miller, P. and Skidmore, P. (2004) *Network Logic*. Demos. (Accessed 03/01/08). http://www.demos.co.uk/publications/networks

Arnstein, S. R. 'A Ladder of Citizen Participation', *Journal of the American Planning Association*, Vol. 35, No. 4, July 1969, pp. 216-224.

Erickson, F. and Schultz, J. (1992). 'Students' experience of the curriculum', in: P. Jackson (ed.), *Handbook of research on curriculum*, New York: Macmillan, pp.464–485.

Moll, L.C., Armanti, C., Neff, D., & Gonzalez, N. (1992). Funds of knowledge for teaching: Using a qualitative approach to connect homes and classrooms. *Theory into Practice,* 31 (2), 132-141.

Moll, L., Gonzalez, N., Amanti, C.(2005) *Funds of Knowledge: Theorizing Practices in Households and Classrooms*, Lawrence Erlbaum Associates Inc, US

Futurelab. *My-E project*. More information can be found at: http://www.futurelab.org.uk/projects/my_e

Department for Children, Schools and Families. *Building Schools for the Future Programme*. More information can be found at: http://www.bsf.gov.uk/

Chapter nine

'Personalised Learning: Taking Choice Seriously'

The Conference Report

by Philip Toogood

The joint conference of Staffordshire University's Creative Communities Unit and the Centre for Personalised Education Trust (trading as Personalised Education Now) was held on 25th June 2007. It was a milestone in the history of education. Its theme, 'Taking Choice Seriously' was derived from the clear notion of personalised education which is being developed and witnessed by the University and Personalised Education Now (PEN).

The conference sent out a call over the landscape of education for the development of a proactive social response to the fundamentally changed situation in industrial society on a global scale. The call went well beyond reactive denigration of governments' panic-stricken efforts to re-enact yesterday's errors as if tomorrow could resurrect a golden age which in fact has never been.

The five main speakers presented a clear message. Wall-charted reactions of the delegates, forum discussions and dialogues, lunch-time networking sessions and afternoon workshops, opened a lively and interactive day of deliberation. Thus the PEN executive committee of Trustees and those attending the conference in effect called for:

- respect to be paid to the informal processes of personal learning;
- support for the human rights of children to learn in a personal manner,
- re-structuring to create the circumstances for self-managed learning;
- technologies of information and communication in the service of learners who are choosing, rather than being forced, to learn.

Clearly and unequivocally the notion of personalised education being the mass customisation of a prescribed curriculum was condemned as a reactionary perversion of the essence of personalised learning. The new dynamic of information technologies being set to serve the same ends of control and domination was also exposed as a blind alley.

In contrast the transformative process of personalised learning within an environment of responsible choice and collaborative learning was defined as an affirmation of the deeper needs of the individual learner to express a personal voice. Customisation of learning, where the notion of personalised education is made to serve the delivery model, was opposed to this transformative process. This transformation, as Mark Webster of the *Creative Communities Unit* at the University of Stafford mentioned in his opening remarks, was effected by the learner engaging in a praxis such as has been described and promoted by Paolo Freire, the Brazilian adult educator and educational philosopher. Freire defined a movement in the learner from awareness-raising, through the stages of researching alternatives, criticising, choice and concluding in action.

The two definitions of personalised learning so fundamentally opposed (transformative and customised) were described in a matrix along two axes intersecting at right angles each of which displayed two poles of a continuum.

One shows the continuum between the poles of the predominance of the *teacher's voice* and at the other extreme *the learner's voice*. The other shows *customisation* at one pole and *transformation* at the other.

The conference was not prescriptive in proposing a single solution. This would not be consistent with the PEN view of personalised learning. This polarisation in education between the teacher and the taught, between formation through customisation and transformation through expression was portrayed as a meaningful framework for describing the field of education.

The conference was not, and was not intended to be, a statement recommending policy moves of a definitive nature (for example the abolition of schools and the substitution of a total home-based education framework). Moving amongst the participants it was possible to detect a whole variety of views concerning reform of the educational system, some more radical than others. This variety was also present in the views of the main speakers. Although PEN promotes research which makes more evident some of the advantages of home-based education and through its association with the inspiring Educational Heretics Press publishing house examines alternatives to the present system and exposes the underlying contradictions and fallacies of systems which adopt the customising version of personalised education, PEN always proceeds in a way which rejects simple (and therefore simplistic) answers to what is a highly complex problem in 'systems' of education.

The intellectual freedom to expose, to consider alternatives, to support the right to opt out of the system and practise otherwise than the conventional wisdom of the day might indicate, is a precious right within our society. The visitor to the first joint conference listening to the speakers and participating in the debates would have been right to reflect on past counter-currents in the European experience of systems of education which even now are enacted in contexts of legal restrictions of choice.

This conference provided a platform for change within and outside 'the system'. As such it was open to people to take a variety of different positions in their particular situations. In the last 50 years there have been movements such as the Community Education movement, the Human Scale Education movement, the Home-based Education movement, Community Arts and Youth Work movement. In addition there has been a growing understanding of how the brain and the emotional side of the human psychology work as well as rapid change in electronic and digital technologies available beyond the book and the oral lecture to use as resources for learning.

In this conference the *Centre for Personalised Education* and the *Creative Communities Unit* are defining the field of personalised learning to enable voices and choices to be raised. The chairperson of PEN, Peter Humphreys, once again spoke of the 'landscape' of personalised education in his opening remarks. Mark Webster, of the *Creative Communities Unit,* Staffordshire University (and author of the inspiring book *Finding Voices: Making Choices*) then provided the facilitator's introduction. The proceedings and inputs of the 5 main speakers which followed, briefly described here, would be well worth collecting in a full publication concerning this conference.

The meaning of the conference was matched by the method behind its organisation. This was not a procession of papers read and left on the table as yet another contribution to the body of intellectual papers based on small corners of research. It was an enjoyable and interactive day in which many voices were raised and heard .

The conference was publicised by the following statement which was carried through in practice:

'Personalised learning has the potential to transform our systems of learning. It challenges the shallow version of learning promoted within the present education system and proposes a new approach where learners themselves make both rational and intuitive choices about their learning. Taking choice seriously is the key driver in this choice. The prize is a cohesive, sustainable and productive society with active and democratically competent citizens.'

The keynote speakers were Tony Jeffs, of Durham University, co-author of the influential book *Informal Education*, Terri Dowty, from *Action on Rights for Children*, Professor Ian Cunningham from the *Centre for Self-Managed Learning* and Dr Tim Rudd from *Futurelab*.

Conference delegates were then able to contribute in a break out session where the challenges in the form of 2 sets of wall charts, one showing the **inhibitors to change** in these directions and the other in the form of the **promoters of change**, were contributed as described below. Key issues were then fed back to the conference.

In the afternoon, after the opportunity for networking and viewing the bookstalls and an excellent buffet lunch, delegates chose between these six workshops:

- The *Otherwise Club* in London, by Leslie Safran
- *My freedom to make choices*, by Alex Dowty, a student delegate
- *Personalised education - a framework for evaluation*, by Peter Humphreys of CPE/PEN
- *Learning Cooperatives*, by Roland Meighan of CPE/PEN
- *The Bridge* - a community group experience of refugees and asylum seekers (a personalised service for people within a hostile culture) by Jackie Rose and Aram Karem
- A *Learning Exchange*, facilitated by Alan Wilkins, consultant in cooperative learning, as an open forum to enable discussion of ideas /issues within the theme of the conference.

Tony Jeffs warned against a definition of personalised learning where the learner, as a discrete unit, learns, or acquires knowledge individually, sitting in front of a computer screen. This misconception merely reflects the malaise in our deeply destroyed society. Like a smoker with emphysema reaching for another cigarette to relieve the distress, we reach for more and more schooling. Those at the conference who lived through the late 70s and 80s when Margaret Thatcher, in line with the classic defence of authoritarianism by Thomas Hobbes in his 'Leviathan', asserted that society did not exist, is an illusion, and that life being 'nasty, brutish and short' we must, therefore, give up our freedom and submit to direction, will shudder at the remembrance of how 'Margaret Thatcher, milk-snatcher', as a young minister of Education, spoke of 'delivering the curriculum'. This ended up with the National Curriculum, SATs and so many other de-personalised features of our education system.

Tony Jeffs called for a personalised education process in society. He envisaged the emergence of vibrant cooperative groups pursuing the real quest for education whose true purpose he defined as the generation of happiness. He spoke of schools as temporary agencies to be replaced by the process of community education in the richness of a new educational society based on democratic principles. He warned that this would be perceived as threatening in our non-democratic society. He asserted that you cannot teach democracy or creativity: you can only draw it out by living it.

He spoke also of the misconception of teaching as delivery of a prescribed curriculum. This was self-defeating since more delivery does not produce more learning. Finland, Sweden and Denmark have the shortest period of schooling and the best results! He called for more self-educating groups and warned against increasing school terms, more compulsory schooling, shorter breaks and longer school days. In UK universities, he said, 49 % of students do not complete their degrees. The roots of this situation were in their earlier school experience, more attuned to recruitment for the army or to be a teacher in the current mould. Significantly, 1 in 3 teachers do not complete the first five years of teaching and leave. By and large new teachers do not know why they are going into teaching and schools were suffering widespread behaviour problems, Ritalin dosage, CCTV cameras and cameras in the classroom. He pointed to Shannon and Rose's research which revealed that levels of literacy in the 1870s and 80s were about the same as today.

The effect of having opted for a low wage low skill economy like the US, was to require generations of 'warehouse' children which would enable marginal workers to work for low pay. Tony Jeffs quoted John Hutton as urging that the only way to eliminate child poverty was to get a second low wage into each household requiring both parents to be at work. This entailed necessarily that their children are 'minded' by schools. In these schools obesity and violence were to be addressed and the 'snake oil' salesmen educational journalists are urging more and more an interpretation of young people as criminals. He spoke also of the dangers of narrow vocationalism in Primary schools. He echoed Henry Morris in this when in his memorandum of 1926 he wrote of the 'dismal dispute of vocational education'. Like Morris he rejected the Gradgrind version of education in which schools were similar to call-centres or Macdonalds. The implication of his comments was similar to that of Henry Morris, that if you get education right in the adult world the you will not have to worry so much about the children.

Turning to adult education and the youth service he revealed the startling statistic that in Norway 1 in 3 adults is involved in a regular study circle. This was by contrast with the in the UK where the narrow vocationalism of many adult education programmes shows how much has been lost in the last 30 years. In the world of youth work he deplored the distortion of youth work as 'personalised into monitoring measurement of young people'. He said crisply that the Guide movement was lacking 20,000 leaders.

His final text for the conference was from Newman, from the 1850s, the era of local Reading Rooms, asserting that education should be inspired by vision and ideas: *'Each one of us has his lamp lit from his neighbour'*. Tony Jeffs sees education as a deep-seated social process within the everyday fabric of our society, rather than as an add-on delivered by schools and other 'temporary' institutions.

Terri Dowty's main concern was with the de-personalising effect of the school system. She spoke of the need for children to have agency over their lives, to be able to question, criticise and challenge. She quoted Jung *"We count for something only because of the essential we embody, and if we do not embody that, life is wasted"*.

She was worried by the use of education by the state as a normative tool. The Extended Schools' Agenda, with recommendations about diet, mental state, friends, habits, could be seen as an attempt by the state to define the 'right person'. In schools 1 in 5 have Special Educational needs and are unable to benefit without extra help. Many did not want to go to school and became potential criminals, pregnant or were unable to go to school and had no job when they finished.

Terri Dowty noted that children who challenge are more able to criticise and be creative in protest, but in one 'beacon' school in Essex a letter went home asking parents to *"discourage children from criticising school at home"*. Children were regimented at school into a curriculum where there is little room for a child's own agenda. Tony Blair was on record as saying that Information Technology enables more personally designed lessons to be prepared! Terri estimated that the school system was letting down at least 50% of children because children do not learn how to ask questions in school circumstances and questioning produces knowledge. One girl was found to be asking questions at home at the rate of 28 per hour whereas at school she only came out with 2! Schools in this sense did not enable education and she called for education to be available, accessible, adaptable and acceptable.

Following these two pleas for an educative community and for children to have more agency over their lives, Ian Cunningham spoke of the work of the *Centre for Self-Managed Learning* to help alienated students at Uckfield Community College to experience personalised education. Small groups of year 8 boys, due to be excluded from school, were remarkably transformed by being in a different, personalised environment for 1½ hours per week. He pointed to a particular problem indirectly, that of teacher as 'front of class performer' and of student as 'empty vessel' to be filled with knowledge as a result of the teacher's performance. He quoted Oscar Wilde who on leaving a theatre performance said *"the performance was a success but the audience was a failure!"* Ian has deep experience of personalised learning at the School of Independent Studies of the former North East London Poly and this lies behind the work of the *Centre for Self-Managed Learning*.

Above all he asserted the importance of group work where people share their knowledge and learning process. He pointed to the contrast with an individualised situation such as personalised learning of a customising sort often set up. In such a situation the sharing would often be described as 'cheating' or 'stealing' other's work and ideas.

He drew up a list of 10 opposed interpretations of features of learning according to the 2 opposed definitions of personalised learning. (see Ch 6)

Tony Jeffs, Terri Dowty and Ian Cunningham stimulated a variety of perceptions about 'Drivers and Barriers' in the development of education towards greater personalisation in a transformative sense. A close study of the returns in the wall-charts showed that these were effectively of 3 sorts:

1. Actual Barriers and Highways (set-ups which lie in the way of or open pathways to change)
2. Inhibitors and Promoters (features which divert/slow up or point to/accelerate the process of change)
3. Threats and Opportunities (forces working against or in favour of change).

No conclusions were put forward at the conference but underlying indications pointed to action being desirable in the following 3 ways:

1. Change the school system,
2. Change the training of teachers from being the 'sage on the stage' to 'guide by the side"
3. Highlight the opportunities for change by intelligent use of the new media and communication technologies.

In answer to the question *'How can we change the system?'* Tim Rudd said that it was apparent that the system was changing itself and that both environmental pressures and ICT advances were enabling moves in this direction. He urged joining the enablers and destroying the impeders to this process! Ian Cunningham said there was a need to look at models of change here and elsewhere. He pointed to a parallel between the last stages of the war in Vietnam when the conventional political message was all about how the war was being won when the real underlying situation was that it had been lost. This tended to re-enforce the statement by Tim Rudd that change was already taking place. Delegates then raised the problem of enabling women to have fulfilling jobs and raise a family in the current economic situation. Terri Dowty responded that there was a great need for advocacy on behalf of poorer families in this respect and urged that the United Nations should enshrine in a civil rights declaration this right for a family to have the opportunity by economic support for the early education of children by the family in the home.

The range of workshops in the afternoon gave outstanding examples of practical initiatives in what was being proposed in the morning talks, wall-chart responses and the pre-lunch forum.

From the point of view of those who were interested in home-based education, the session facilitated by Leslie Saffron, the founder and coordinator of the *Otherwise Club* in London was exemplary. Here, it seems, is the answer to those who denigrate home-based education, showing how it is possible, within a community developing framework for families to organise cooperative and collaborative learning at and from home and to have the best of all worlds in making sure that not only is education dedicated to the generation of happiness but also that there are other pathways to qualifications where necessary which can be supported by socially innovatory centres such as the *Otherwise Club*.

The other workshops were equally interesting in their different fields and these examples of good practice will be included in a fuller publication resulting from this conference: Workshop facilitation by Alex Dowty from his own experience of the freedom outside the schools system to make choices; by Peter Humphreys on an 'evaluation framework' from his own work as Chair of PEN; by Roland Meighan about 'Learning Cooperatives'; by workers at *The Bridge* providing personalised service for refugees and asylum seekers in our country; and facilitation of a broad learning exchange on the theme of the conference by such an experienced expert as Alan Wilkins, were a sparkling range of offers in the afternoon.

The final presentation, after the workshops, was by Tim Rudd of *Futurelab*. *Futurelab* is dedicated to finding and producing creative solutions to the opportunity of the new Information and Communication Technology in education and learning. He supported wholeheartedly the use of ICT for transformational purposes in the field of personalised learning. He called for an innovative focus rather than for the use of computers in schools to be dedicated to the achievement of a set of pre-defined, deliverable targets. He wanted people to be able to develop their own learning, making choices and finding their voice. He saw learners as subjects rather than as objects. He wanted less prescription and more active dialogue, support for diversity and participation by the learner towards empowerment, autonomy and ownership in a changed relationship with teachers. Here Tim Rudd produced a diagram of the personalisation continuum. He pointed to the need for appropriate skills of learning in the 21st century and for the participation of the learner in the learning process. He talked of the ladder of participation by the learner in this process, from the non-participation of didactic teaching, through token participation to the learner empowerment of personalised education in a transformative sense.

Finally, it was significant that the conference was sensitively hosted by the *Creative Communities Unit* of the University of Staffordshire and that this growing partnership with PEN is being led by Mark Webster who brings a Community Arts perspective to the job. The intellectual openness and precision of Dr. Roland Meighan and the long experience of Janet Meighan in Early Childhood education and in administrative support for *Personalised Education Now* helped to make this such an enjoyable day.

However, the tireless work of Peter Humphreys in sustaining the PEN/CPE Trust , which he modestly concealed, and his inspirational dedication to keeping the disparate elements of the movement for personalised education focused on a broad landscape, should receive a special mention and thanks from all those attending this conference.

Contributors

Mark Webster from *Staffordshire University's Creative Communities Unit* is a senior Lecturer in the Faculty of Arts Media and Design.

Tony Jeffs teaches at *Durham University* he is a member of the Community and Youth Work Studies Unit. His research interests are in the areas of Youth Policy, Informal Education and Community Work.

Peter Humphreys is the Chair of the *Centre for Personalised Education Trust.* He has had a 25 year primary teaching career and has interests in ICT and its potential to transform learning systems and enable learner choice.

Alan Wilkins is a consultant on Co-operative Learning with over 25 years experience in learning and development. He has worked in secondary and further education institutions, a local education authority and a range of co-operative enterprises.

Dr. Roland Meighan now works as a writer and publisher. Previously he was Senior Lecturer in Education at the University of Birmingham for 20 years and then Special Professor of Education at *Nottingham University*. He is a specialist on learning systems.

Leslie Barson founded and continues to run *The Otherwise Club*, 'a home-based education invitational learning community', in NW London. Her two children now aged 19 and 25 have never been to school. Her PhD thesis investigates how home-based education affects parents.

Professor Ian Cunningham chairs Strategic Developments International Ltd and the *Centre for Self-Managed Learning,* an educational charity. He is Visiting Professor in Organisational Capability at Middlesex University and a Visiting Fellow in the Centre for Educational Innovation at the University of Sussex.

Jackie Rose, is a Research Officer with the Creative Communities Unit and member of the *Bridge International Youth* Project, which engages young asylum seekers and refugees in a programme of personal support, arts, educational and cultural activities and community integration.

Dr Tim Rudd is Senior Researcher in *Futurelab's* learning team. He is currently leading on a range of educational technology research and development projects within *Futurelab*. Previously he was Head of Evidence and Research at BECTA.

Philip Toogood is a consultant in mini schooling and flexi-schooling. Following a long career in education as teacher and headteacher in a variety of settings, which included a parent-teacher co-operative small school and Flexi-college.

Centre for Personalised Education Trust (CPE)

CPE is a charitable company whose trading name is **Personalised Education Now (PEN).** It promotes education based on learner-managed learning, using a flexible catalogue curriculum, located in a variety of settings, and operating within a framework of democratic values and practices. It is a membership organization which publishes a Journal, Newsletters, E-briefings, and maintains a website,
www.c.person.ed.gn.apc.org